An Ordered Life

The Andrew N. Nelson Story

By

Dorothy Minchin-Comm

and

Dorothy Nelson-Oster

2010

DeeEzBee
graphics©2010
Debi S Barnhart
Riverside, CA
e-mail: debimathewb
@charter.net

Order this book online at www.trafford.com
or email orders@trafford.com

Most Trafford titles are also available at major online book retailers.

Printed in the United States of America.

ISBN: 978-1-4269-4923-4 (sc)

Trafford rev. 12/20/2010

www.trafford.com

North America & International
toll-free: 1 888 232 4444 (USA & Canada)
phone: 250 383 6864 ♦ fax: 812 355 4082

Cover Art

The *SS Adriatic*, the first steamship of the White Star Line, was built in 1871. Anders Nelson and Gustava Jonson sailed on this ship from Liverpool to New York in 1886. Being heavily clad with iron (even the decks were iron) and capable of high speeds, the *Adriatic* had been involved in several serious accidents. While some considered it a predatory—even a cursed—ship, for the young couple from Sweden the journey was the beginning of their courtship and the doorway to a new life in America.

(Painting by: George Parker Greenwood (1889), Wikipedia, in public domain. The print was reversed for the cover at author's request.)

Dedication

To all of the generations of the family of

1208 Shelby Street, Seattle,

who have followed in the tradition of

Andrew and Vera Nelson

and have

served in foreign mission fields.

Preface

For many years, the Andrew N. Nelson story has been "waiting in the wings" to be written. Details of a life so well and so enthusiastically lived should not be lost. Consequently, if even one undecided, unfulfilled young person or one disillusioned, discouraged adult could take one step nearer to knowing his God, Andrew would have been satisfied.

The writing of the book was dependent upon three members of the Nelson family. Credit goes:

To Dorothy Nelson-Oster (daughter), for deciding to honor her father with the writing of his story. She harvested information from his diaries and letter-files, all of which filled out the details of his well-ordered life. (Fragments of his original writings appear in quotation marks.) Articles published in Seventh-day Adventist church papers also helped to document the chronology of his life.

To Richard Nelson (son), for reading the manuscript day by day and for remembering high lights of his father's life. And Donald Nelson (son) for sharing his reminiscences.

To Mitzi Smith-Wiggle (niece), for finishing the tales collected by her mother Vivian Nelson-Smith-Cushman, *Stories from the Family of 1208*. Mitzi continues the task as historian of the Nelson family and has provided most of the photographs that appear. She happily consented to proofread the text.

Finally, Debi Barnhart prepared this book for publication.

Dorothy Minchin-Comm PhD
Professor of English (Ret.)
La Sierra University, Riverside, CA
December 2010

Table of Contents

Andrew Nathaniel Nelson

1. Dead Men Walking

Andrew Nelson looked at his watch as he waited in the Death House at New Bilibid Prison near Manila. Four o'clock in the morning. Already he'd walked thirteen Japanese prisoners-of-war to the gallows. One more to go. Outside, the constant drizzling rain, the heavy clouds, and the sickly warm air challenged a disheartened half-moon.

Although the Philippine Army had conducted the executions with all possible decency, the horror of it all still lay like a dagger to the heart. The U. S. Army had turned these war-trial cases over to the Philippine Government. Understandably, the Filipinos had a long, long account to settle with the Japanese.

The prisoners had not been told that this night of January 19, 1951, was their night to die. Only after Dr. Nelson had arrived at the prison had Warden Alfredo Bunye called the men to his office to announce the executions. They never returned to their cells.[1]

A long-time missionary in the Far East and a member of General MacArthur's occupation and reconstruction forces in Japan, Nelson had still never before attended an execution. He had been ministering to these men as prison chaplain for more than two years, while he served as president of Philippine Union College. Four of them he knew and loved as Christian brothers, and the pain of it all plummeted him into a state of near shock.[2] Some of the men, he knew with certainty, were innocent of the war crimes with which they had been charged.

Nonetheless, all had moved forward with inexorable precision. Nelson had ridden with each prisoner in the dimly lighted death wagon. He had stood at the foot of the gallows as each man ascended the thirteen steps. Each time, after the trap door had sprung open, the executioners carried the body out to the mass grave. Then Andrew Nelson returned to the Death House to walk the next prisoner on his "Last Mile." The next hanging could not take place until the previous one was complete. Thus, the executions proceeded at thirty-minute intervals.

Andrew sighed with the most complete and utter exhaustion he'd ever known. The night had been excruciatingly long and overwhelmingly sad. At 9:30 p.m. the first officer began to walk *his* last mile. A Buddhist, the distraught man could comprehend nothing of the kind of hope that Andrew tried to offer him. Mercifully, when he reached the top of the thirteen steps, he fainted and knew nothing more of what happened to him.

The next was Captain Heidiachi Nakamura. He'd been among the first of the Japanese prisoners to become a Seventh-day Adventist Christian. Both he and Dr. Nelson knew that he was innocent of the crime. On his last walk he talked calmly of his wife and ten-year-old son back in Japan. At the top of the steps, Nakamura looked down at Andrew: *"Oyasumi nasai. Ashita mata omeni kakarimasu"* ("Goodnight. I'll see you in the morning.") Those final words became a kind of formula that Andrew used throughout the long killing hours that night.

Some of the prisoners understood the meaning. Others did not. Back at the death house the Buddhists sat with their priest, intoning prayers and incantations. Sometimes angry voices punctuated the murky stillness.

Meanwhile, Nakamura had stood tall, not a trace of the criminal anywhere about him. The doctors took his blood pressure and fingerprinted him (again), measures that Andrew considered utterly useless. Then the Captain firmly walked up the steps. The knot was adjusted and a black hood pulled over his head. All the while he was praying. The strong, beautiful prayer in Japanese speech rang out in the night, understood by no one else present but Dr. Nelson. It had been the courageous, spontaneous, very personal cry of faith from a heart that, just moments later, would stop.

The trap door snapped, and a good man's life ended. The head of the prison guard sent a corporal over to Nelson. "What did he say?" Chaplain Nelson was more than pleased to interpret the prayer.

"Was he a Christian, then?" someone else asked.

"Well, anyway, I waited until he said 'Amen,'" the corporal muttered defensively.

"A Christian he was indeed!" Nelson spoke with intense pride.

In due course, another prisoner had arrived. An avowed atheist, this one needed nothing from Dr. Nelson. He did, however, hand him a beautiful but fatalistic poem that he'd written, while waiting his turn.

Finally, Andrew walked the last mile with Captain Sueo Abe, another earnest (though very new) Christian. The ride in the death-wagon even seemed to make Abe cheerful. "You know, Pastor Nelson," He grinned from ear to ear. "I am so happy about one thing. Tobacco was a demon in my life, but I got the victory, didn't I?"

"That you did, Brother Abe."

"Now," he sighed, "I am clean! Clean!" He climbed the steps and smiled down at Andrew one more time. "Goodnight. I'll see you in the morning." Then, Captain Abe, so full of faith and vitality, was gone.

When Nelson turned his little black Chrysler back toward the campus of Philippine Union College, the sun had not yet even grayed the dark sky that still oozed rain. Never had he endured such a night. Fourteen men were not even cold in their grave, and he was the last human being they had seen or spoken to.

What had he done for those prisoners?

He'd shown them Christ. When Jesus died as a poor peasant, crucifixion and injustice were tragically common. So common as to scarcely raise a comment. Having walked this path Himself, Jesus showed us all the way. Down through the ages whenever a believer has died, He is right there to travel through the Valley with him or her. He consoles us. And He promises us that death will not—cannot—have the final victory over us.[3]

How did Andrew Nelson, at age fifty-eight, come to find himself in these traumatic circumstances on a steamy hot night in Manila?

Well, that's the rest of the story. It all began with a leap into destiny, without which there never could have been a Dr. Andrew N. Nelson.

[1] Andrew N. Nelson, "The Last Mile," (Unpublished Manuscript), pp. 49-54.
[2] Four Seventh-day Adventists were executed in Bilibid Prison. *North Philippine Union Gleaner* (September 24, 1951), p. 1.
[3] Andrew Greeley, *Jesus: A Meditation on His Stories and His Relationship with Women.* (New York: A Tom Doherty Assoc. Book, c 2007), p. 166.

2. The Leap into Destiny

Anders Nelson[1] was born in Janstorp on May 27, 1865, a tiny village southeast of the old university town of Lund. He had been preceded by eight siblings, including two baby girls who died in infancy. Benedicta, Maria, Anna, Jons, Lars, and Kjesti came before Anders, and one more little brother, Sven, followed. Sadly, the premature death of the last child embittered Anders' father, especially against the clergy. (It didn't help that the priest was a drunkard.)

Anders himself remained very conscientious all of his life. He was confirmed in the Lutheran Church, despite the fact that the priest instructing the class was often drunk and sometimes didn't show up at all. As a very small boy, he tried one alcoholic drink, but it burned his throat so severely that he never drank again, ever.

Although Skania, the southernmost province of Sweden, was the country's largest agricultural area, Anders' father Nils Swantrom was no farmer. He much preferred reading. Meanwhile, his capable wife Kama, with help of two *pigas* (servant girls) ran the water-powered mill and a bakery in the town. The family's circumstances, however, deteriorated rapidly. Eventually they lost all of their property and moved to Staffanstorp.

At eight years of age, Anders hired out to work as a *drang* (farmhand). He began caring for geese and then moved on to horses and cows in his teen years. If he'd ever acquired the income, he would have bought a little farm. At a mere 25 *kroner* a year, however, he knew he'd never attain that dream.

Then, Anders heard that bricklayers knew how to be wealthy. "Yes, we get good wages, but we cannot work in cold, wet weather," one of them told him. Next, his mother suggested, "Let's write to your brother Jons in Vimmerby. You could learn to be a cabinet maker." Thus followed Anders' three-year apprenticeship to his brother Jons.

During this time, he developed into a kind of "odd-ball" by refusing to get drunk with the other apprentices in town. He even signed a temperance pledge at the local Baptist church. Moreover, he didn't gamble either. A very peculiar kind of young man.

When his apprenticeship ended in the spring of 1886, Anders left the home of his brother Jons and his wife Alida. Where was he going to find money to buy tools and materials? In passing, he wondered about their older brother Lars. No one had heard much of anything from him since he'd left for "Amerika." Then at this crucial moment in Anders' life there suddenly came a fascinating piece of mail. It contained money for a boat ticket. "Come at once and join me in this country," Lars wrote,

Anders immediately recognized the opportunity. The doors to a new life had suddenly been flung open before him. Eyes alight with enthusiasm, he glimpsed a future urgently beckoning him to come.

Jons and Alida received his announcement with steady logic. "But you're of age now, and you haven't yet done your compulsory military service."

"I know." Briefly Anders wished that he'd submitted to that dreary obligation sooner. No matter. "But now I can buy the ticket," Anders replied. "I can go to Maria's home in Lund while I wait to find a ship going to Amerika. It's near Malmo."

"But her husband is a policeman. Hans Mattsson will report you, sure thing," Jons countered. "You'll get arrested. In fact, the army camp is on the way to Malmo."

"I must go. I'll need a little trunk to pack my things." Anders was adamant. "Don't you see?" They could see all right. Their inventive brother would not be deterred. Not even by the prison-time that awaited him if he was caught in his attempt to escape to America.

"Well, then," Jons said, "I shall have to go with you. We can walk to the train station beyond the army base and then buy your ticket. Otherwise the army recruiters will certainly spot you. You look like a teenager."

Anders stayed with the Hans Mattssons on Mariagatan Street in Lund. He visited some of the places he'd worked in his farmhand days, walking everywhere to avoid undue attention. Coincidentally, the town motto of Lund was: *"Ideernas Stad"* ("City of Ideas"). Although Anders had not studied at the famous old University, he certainly was not short on ideas. As for scholarship, that would work itself out quite magnificently in the very next generation of his family

Daily Anders scanned the sailing notices in the Malmo newspaper *Sydsvenska Dagbladet* until he found a ship bound for New York. The *SS Adriatic* was the White Star Line's first steamship and would be sailing out of Liverpool.[2] A smaller vessel out of Malmo would get him across to England.

The capital of Skåne County, Malmo had long lived off its shipbuilding yards and related industries. While in the White Star ticket office Anders saw a beautiful girl standing in line. She turned around and smiled at him.

The plot intensified. Anders and his brother-in-law Hans stayed in Malmo for two days. Sunday morning they went to the dock warehouse. Anders hid among the boxes, trunks and other cargo, while Hans stood watching the passengers board the ship.

"You *must* stay in hiding until I blow my whistle. If you're recognized you'll be sent off to army training instantly." Standing there by the gangplank, Hans Mattsson in his uniform blended in well with the departure scene, and no one took notice of him.

The ropes were lifted off the wharf moorings, and the gangplank went up. Slowly the ship edged away. At the last possible moment, Hans gave his whistle one sharp toot. Catapulting out of the shed, Anders loped across the pier and threw his trunk onto the deck. With a mighty leap, he cleared the ever-widening margin of water, now a full yard wide. His long, lean legs landed him safely beside his trunk. Both Anders and Hans heaved great sighs of relief as they turned and waved to one another.

Anders did possess a legitimate ticket for his journey to America, his unusual embarkation notwithstanding. Once cleared of suspicion, he went to locate his bunk. Down there in steerage, he saw that pretty girl again and discovered that her name was Gustava Jonson. Together they went back up on deck to watch the coast of Sweden fade into the eastern horizon. Although strangers, they wept a little together over leaving their homeland. Secretly, Gustava comforted herself with the idea that she'd earn some money and then return to Sweden. She gave herself three years.

Anders was going to learn a lot about little Gustava. He immediately set about getting acquainted.

Born in the village of Byrnakulla (*Byrn* "bears" and *kulla* "hill"), Gustava had been christened in its little white-steepled *kyrka* ("church") on December 5, 1866. Her mother, Assrina Bengstad, already had Christina, a six-year-old daughter, when her new baby arrived. Her father, John Oberg, a house painter who lived next door, married Assrina. The whole family moved together into the servant's room off the kitchen where she worked as a *piga* (cook and housekeeper).

Gustava was only four years old when her father died of lead poisoning. All she could remember of his deteriorating mental and physical health was that one morning he went out and painted the household pig green!

Her elementary schooling was free, but high school was not. Therefore, both girls went no further than grade eight. Their mother had no money to pay for further education. While Mama liked to have her daughters read the newspaper to her, they suspected that she herself was illiterate. Like her, both Christina and Gustava appeared to be destined to live in poverty as *pigas*.

Nonetheless, six-year-old Gustava began school with a passion for learning. She loved to study and discover the world beyond Byrnakulla. Even beyond Sweden. She always admired her teachers extravagantly. When describing it all to her children, she would exclaim, "I was always top of the class! I wanted to be a teacher." Eyes shining, she would add, "And when we played games, I was the best!"

She had to take her first *piga* job in Helsingborg, thirty miles from Byrnakulla. Two months later her mother Assrina died. Desolate, Gustava wept inconsolably. "Stop crying and get your work done," her employer snarled. "You're only a *piga* and always will be." (A day would come when Gustava, in her comfortable home overlooking the bay in Seattle, would appreciate the irony of that nasty remark.)

In the Lutheran church confirmation always marked induction into adulthood. Being of a very religious turn of mind, Gustava learned all of her Bible stories. For a lifetime, she would maintain friendships with people she met there, including the nine youngsters in her confirmation class. Especially her Sunday School teacher Ellen Nelson. (Out of respect, she called *Moster*, "mother's sister," Ellen.)

After *Moster* Ellen and her niece Natalja left for America, Gustava did find better *piga* work with a kindly sea captain and his wife, also in Helsingborg.

When her sister Christina sent her money to buy a boat ticket to America, however, the captain had nothing good to say about the proposition. Because he'd been all over the world, Gustava at first half believed him. "It's the thieves, robbers and murderers who are all going to Amerika," he warned.

The fatherly captain also advised her against *any* men who "were likely to cause trouble." When she and Anders first met aboard ship, of course, Gustava had no idea exactly *how* Anders was leaving Sweden. His method *could* be interpreted as causing trouble.

Alone and without family or friends, however, what did she have to stay back for? Therefore, she'd gone off to secure her exit visa from the church census priest. Apart from her precious doll the little trunk she bought was the first thing she'd ever really owned. It was just 36 x 20 x 24 inches, but it held everything she possessed. It even had a rounded top to accommodate a lady's hat. *Pigas*, however, were not allowed to wear hats, so Gustava didn't have one.   (One of the first defiant moves she made, upon arriving at her destination in Kansas City, was to buy a hat!)

That day at the White Star Office in Malmo, the line of passengers moved very slowly. Almost 100 young Swedes were leaving their homeland in search of a better life in America. The local newspaper complained: "Today (May 16, 1886) ninety-nine Swedes turned their backs against their fatherland and left for Amerika."

Gustava looked anxiously around her. Which ones were the robbers and murderers? One tall, blond youth with piercing blue eyes smiled at her. She smiled back.

By the time the ship from Malmo reached Hull on the east coast of England, Anders and Gustava had, at least, become acquainted. They went by train to Liverpool where they walked the streets, absorbing their first impressions of the world outside of their tiny bit of Sweden. Anders met a church pastor there who told him to invite all the young Swedes traveling to America. "Tell them to come to our Sunday evening service." Anders tried, but everyone said, "No thanks! We've had enough religion already." Only Gustava attended church with him.

Walking back to their lodgings from the evening service, Anders and Gustava actually had a deep, spiritual conversation. They agreed to write to one another. When she gave him her address with Christina and Moster Ellen in Kansas City, Anders put the paper in his pocket reverently. "I will be as careful of this as if it were money!"

As the passengers boarded the *Adriatic* for the Atlantic crossing, most of them had to face the very inferior realities of "steerage class." All poor immigrants could afford only the lowest possible fares. The great open space of the hold was fitted out with bunks stacked nine high. Each person's bed measured 3' wide by 7' long.

Anders noted how modestly Gustava pinned her sheets around her bunk for privacy. Everyone shared the same area, and the women were required to go to bed one hour ahead of the men—with some of the sailors offering far more help than was required. Another section of the hold was filled with black pigs that emitted sound effects and a powerfully bad smell.

By and large, Anders kept to himself on the ship. He'd just left his dearly loved mother, and he didn't know any of the other young people. The walk that he and Gustava took back to the ship from the church service in Liverpool, however, came as a real wake-up call for him. Never before had he had such a conversation with a girl! Or with anyone else, for that matter.

The steerage passengers on the *Adriatic* spent as much of the long summer days on deck as they possibly could. Anders took every opportunity to watch the very fetching little Gustava.

[1] For many years many members of Andrew N. Nelson's ancestral family had used "Swanstrom" (the name of their step-grandfather) as their surname. Most of those who emigrated to the United States reverted to the original name of "Nelson."
[2] The *Adriatic's* maiden voyage across the Atlantic began on April 11, 1872. With four masts, one funnel it was 452 feet long and had a service speed of 14.5 knots. It carried 1,200 passengers, with 1,000 of them in steerage.

3. A Foothold in the Promised Land

The *Adriatic* arrived in New York on July 3, 1886. Since it was a holiday weekend, the shores looked bright with flags flying. Everything felt festive, as a true "Promised Land" should do. Although the ship docked on Saturday, the passengers did not disembark until the next day. It had been forty-nine days since Anders had taken that leap into destiny off the Malmo dock and had landed, so to speak, at Gustava's feet.

This day both Anders and Gustava (temporarily) changed their nationality. They went through the official immigration center, Castle Garden, an old fort in Battery Park, at the southern tip of Manhattan.[1] At a time when travel documents were often sketchy, no one questioned them when they listed themselves as coming from Denmark. Anders (now Andrew) had a lurking fear that somehow, the long arm of the Swedish military might still reach out and seize him.

After all, Skåne had once belonged to Denmark (until 1677). Andrew knew that from the top of Sankt Hans Hill in Lund you could *see* Copenhagen. Ferries constantly crossed and re-crossed the Oresund Strait. (Today the Oresund Bridge provides a five-mile-long land-link between Denmark and Sweden.) Besides, he and Gustava had relatives—albeit distant ones—in Denmark. Therefore, on July 4, 1886, at Castle Garden both Andrew and Gustava were Danish.[2]

Andrew had had his twenty-first birthday aboard the *Adriatic* soon after she put to sea. Already he was quite sure that he wanted to marry the nineteen-year-old Gustava. She, however, arrived at her decision in her own time.

Carrying their little trunks, Andrew and Gustava walked a half-mile to the railway station. As the train moved west, they marveled at the celebrations in every little town—picnics, games, flags and speeches. What a country, they mused. "A feast every day!"

They parted in Pittsburgh, Pennsylvania. Andrew boarded the train to meet his brother Lars Swanstrom in Helena, Montana, and Gustava headed south to join Christina and Moster Ellen in Kansas City Missouri.

In Kansas City, Gustava happily found herself earning $25 a month rather than per year. In fact, after using equipment and preparing foods she'd never seen before, she rose to the station of a "chief cook." She joined the Lutheran Church and soon made many friends there. She liked the pastor. He was so different from the priest she'd known back in Sweden.

Andrew's 6,000-mile trip finally ended in Helena in the Territory of Montana. Upon arrival he asked for "Lars Swanstrom." No one knew of such a person, so Andrew settled down to wait. The stationmaster eyed him carefully throughout the afternoon and detected a family resemblance. Finally, he announced, "I'll take you to your brother. His name is now Charley Nelson." The reunion of the brothers was happy enough, but no one really knew how to make him welcome because he didn't smoke, chew tobacco or drink!

Although Andrew never saw his homeland again, he never forgot his heritage. There was a large Scandinavian community in Chicago and he subscribed to two Swedish newspapers from there. Sometimes he even contributed local immigrant news to them. Meanwhile, he used every job he got to improve his command of English. In addition to some time in a gold mine, he worked on several farms and cared for horses.

Then his career became more focused. Together Andrew and Charley sent money to bring Jons and his family to America. Working again with his skilled brother, Andrew now learned carpentry. Together they were hired at St. Peter's Mission for Indian Children near Cascade.

At last, Andrew could dispatch the letter he'd been waiting to write to Gustava. "I have a job, and I'll send you money. Now you can come to Montana and marry me."

Her reply shocked him. "No. You must come to Kansas City so that we can get better acquainted." Clearly, she was looking for something more secure than a shipboard romance and was insisting on a "proper" courtship.

Determined never to "miss a boat"—and certainly not this one–

Andrew promptly took off for Kansas. He soon found employment finishing the interiors and building the benches for the new horse-drawn streetcars in the city. He also made furniture for the prisoners at Fort Leavenworth.

The intervening three years had changed nothing. Andrew and Gustava discovered that their feelings for one another remained absolutely valid. On December 17, 1889, they became engaged. Andrew presented his fiancée with a beautiful leather-bound Bible. Both of them wrote on the dedication page, solemnly committing their lives to God and to one another.

Together they regularly attended the Lutheran Church, until the day that Gustava raised a question about baptism. The priest airily dismissed the subject: "Oh, when people get worried about baptism, they just go over and join the Baptist Church."

The couple began attending that church and were baptized together in May, 1890. For Andrew's birthday that month Gustava gave him a copy of *Bible Readings for the Home Circle*, sold to her by a fine young Christian youth who showed up at her door. Neither of them could yet foresee the ultimate implications of that event in their lives.

In fact, Andrew had been seriously put off by the local town drunk, an odious old Swede. One day he found the disreputable fellow on the street, well dressed and coherent. "I am now a Seventh-day Adventist," he told Nelson.

Although the evidence before his eyes was amazing, Andrew still didn't want anything to do with the man–especially when the enthusiastic, regenerated fellow kept urging his new faith upon him, unbidden.

For the present Andrew and Gustava faced a more pressing question. Should they settle in Missouri or Montana? Andrew really wanted to be near his brothers again. With Jons he could *really* learn how to build houses. Moreover, Montana had just become a state. On July 13, 1891, he headed back north.

By October, Andrew was back with Jons at the Mission and was able to send for his bride. They decided to marry the day she arrived in Helena, October 23. Gustava repacked her trunk and said goodbye to her friends. Leaving Moster Ellen was the hardest part of separation. She, after all, went back to her "*piga*" days in Helsingborg.

Her train journey north involved a layover in Green River,

Wyoming, and Gustava spent her "wedding day" alone. Meanwhile, her bridegroom kept meeting every train that came into Helena.

Fortunately, the bride arrived safely the next day. They settled her luggage in the rooming house and secured the marriage license. Andrew had a bouquet of lily-of-the-valley for her when they presented themselves to the Baptist pastor. They asked an affable bystander to be the witness and were forthwith married. "That was the best thing I ever did," Andrew exulted in his memoir. "I married a jewel."[3]

Gustava had barely turned Andrew's wretched little log cabin in Cascade into something like a real home when the government closed the Mission down. They packed up and faced another decision. Should they go south to Helena or north to Great Falls. Although they prayed about it, the couple had no firm conviction about what they should do. At the Cascade railway station they decided to board the first train that came, whether it went north or south. The first one carried them up to Great Falls.

They found it a lively, growing town (population 2,500). Within twenty-four hours Andrew had found work. Their neat little home quickly became the center for all of the Swedish young people, most of them connected with the Baptist Church.

When a tent was pitched down by the river, the evangelistic meetings attracted many young people. At first, people thought it was a circus, but the director turned out to be a Seventh-day Adventist preacher, not a clown. Andrew had already encountered one Adventist in Kansas City and was cautious. When religious discussions broke out in her house, poor Gustava retreated to her kitchen and shut the door. "What I don't know, I won't be held responsible for," she said to herself. For the time being, the matter was shelved, and life in Great Falls proceeded pleasantly enough.

Two years later, the United States was caught up in The Great Panic of 1893, the worst the country had ever seen up to that time. The railroads had overbuilt with shaky financing, and bankruptcies exploded almost overnight. While huge fortunes were being made, the country still plunged into an economic depression. Banks and stores closed their doors, and the silver mines and smelters stopped. Plenty of work to be done, but no one had any money to pay salaries.

Early that year Gustava was happily pregnant. One day she and Andrew walked downtown to see a new invention. The Singer Sewing Machine Company had opened a shop on the main street.

Gustava eagerly followed the salesman's demonstration. They paid $50.00, for a model housed in a beautiful oak cabinet and went home dreaming of the many hours of time it would save. It represented an enormous outlay of cash, but they courageously plunged ahead.

Amid all of this stress, personal and public, Andrew and Gustava found great comfort in the birth of their first baby, Andrew Nathaniel, born on December 23, 1893. They were so happy and so proud of their handsome little boy that they weathered the Panic better than many of their neighbors did.

Their own Panic came a few months later, when Gustava found Baby Andrew crying, stretching, and jerking his arms and legs in an odd way. He didn't want to nurse. Papa Andrew rushed out to find a doctor.

"Your child is very ill," the medical man told them. "He's having convulsions. He'll probably have a few more, and then his heart will stop. Nothing can be done." The doctor rose to leave.

Terrified, the young parents fell to their knees, pleading for healing for their child. Alone but together, they watched the spasms recede. They shared the joy [of] this miracle with their good friends at their Baptist church.

Early on, Andrew N's propensity for mischief became legendary. His mother was quite ill during her second pregnancy,[4] but he cut her no slack. He gathered up every tool he could find in the kitchen, ending with a scuttle full of coal with which he dusted himself, his white dress, and most of the house. She had to give up on resting.

One morning Andrew helped Mama by carrying a pancake to give to his father. It fell to the floor. Without hesitation the toddler picked it up, restored it to the plate, and served it to his father. "Oh, well," Anders thought to himself, "Mama always keeps the floor clean." He pleased his son greatly by promptly eating the offering.

Young Andrew soon showed an acute awareness of the fine points of language. Gustava taught him a short poem to recite at a special service at church. Since he was a such a cute, friendly little fellow, she knew that the church members would enjoy hearing him. Beforehand, she even took him to the empty church to practice. Then, she thought, he'll be at ease in the big room. He recited the poem perfectly several times. "What a good boy!" she exclaimed.

Mind at ease, Gustava took him back to church the next Sunday.

He marched confidently up to the platform, just as he'd been taught. His mother waited. The whole congregation waited. Andrew stared severely at them all. Mama prompted him with the first word or two. Still not a word from Andrew. Then he turned directly to his mother, waving his arm in a wide circle, "If all of these people go away, then I'll say my poem."

A couple of years later, Anders and Gustava became aware of the potential hazards of bilingualism. One day, Andrew accompanied his Papa to a job-site. He stood watching his father use a hammer to knock down an old building. When a man stopped to watch, Andrew explained, "*Vi* are *riving* down dis *vag*." ("We're tearing down this wall.")

Although Andrew had achieved what appeared to be a perfectly reasonable blend of Swedish and English, he had difficulty. Because the boy was obviously very intelligent, at age six he went off to Grade 1. He would love it. And so he did. Within a couple of weeks, however, he brought home a note from the teacher. "Andrew needs to learn more English. Please keep him home until the next session begins."

A wake-up call for Anders and Gustava Nelson! They were indeed in "Amerika," and they needed to use more English. No one could foresee it at the time, but Andrew would never again have a set-back in language use. Not ever, for the rest of his life.

Although the Nelsons had been living in Great Falls for some years, Anders began to rationalize. By now he and Gustava had four children: Andrew (9), Gertrude (7), Philip (5) Reuben (3). To be sure, it was time to find a permanent home. In the milder climate on the coast he could continue his construction work in that green land the year round. Forthwith he set out on a reconnaissance trip to Seattle. There he bought a lot on 2317 Federal Avenue and began to build a house. A long, narrow one in the woods pressed up against a hillside. Rather awkwardly, the kitchen had to be remote at one end of the building.

Before she could leave Great Falls, Gustava had to sell four houses and two rentals. When all was done, Andrew and his siblings, Gertrude, Philip, and Reuben, found the 600-mile train trip to Seattle great fun. They arrived in May, 1904, and moved into a rented apartment while Anders finished the new little house for them.

Andrew proudly worked along with his father on the building.

In the woods the kids played hide-and-seek, picked flowers and ate wild berries. Genuine live Indians lived just over the hill, they discovered. Their front-yard view reached all the way to Lake Union (now called Portage Bay) and the new University of Washington. Above all, the house had real electricity! The Baptist Sunday School and the Baptist College were just one convenient block away. In due course, someone built a larger house right in front of the little Nelson house.

In any case, the growing family needed more space. Therefore, Andrew secured another wooded lot overlooking Lake Union. While he worked other jobs, it took him a while to build a lovely big house at 2337 North Broadway. Finally, they moved in.

Almost immediately a new challenge arose. The Sletingren family lived next door to the Nelson home. The two houses shared a water meter. One Friday evening Papa Nelson came into the kitchen. "Mama, do you have three dollars? Our water bill's due today, and I don't want Mrs. Sletingren to think that we're careless about paying bills."

Mrs. Sletingren met Andrew at the door. "I'm sorry," she said. "The sun is down, and Sabbath has begun. I can't take your money now."

"And you're right, ma'am!" Nelson tipped his hat, turned on his heel and went home.

Back in the kitchen, he returned the money to his wife. She looked at her somewhat pale-faced husband. "Are they Advents then?"

Andrew nodded, "Yes." So they'd moved all the way from Montana to get away from the arguments of those fanatical Adventists! Now they'd built a new house right next door to another batch of them.

Meanwhile, Mrs. Sletingren had heard Andrew say, "You're right!" She lost no time. At church the next day she reported an interesting piece of news to Mrs. Cox: "My new neighbor already knows which day is the Sabbath."

All along the way, however, Mama Nelson had been less convinced of this Bible truth than her husband. Therefore the Sletingrens set up regular Bible studies for Gustava. She always took both her Swedish and English Bibles when she went next door to meet the Bible teacher. At first she didn't want to go, but she didn't want to be rude to her new neighbors.

At the end of each of the weekly Bible studies, she'd call the children into their own parlor to share with them what she'd learned that day. Meanwhile, every time she talked about a new idea, her husband just said, "I know that."

Finally Mama decided to read through the whole New Testament to find the text that authorized the change of the Sabbath to Sunday. She couldn't find it. "Well," she said to herself, "someone more educated than I am would surely know where it is.

Forthwith, she planned a special tea for the three Swedish Baptist pastors in town. Surely, all together, they would know. After serving the tea and cakes and enjoying a brief visit, she explained the reason for the party. "Please show me in the Bible the text that says that the Sabbath was changed from Saturday to Sunday."

Suddenly, the atmosphere of the cozy little gathering changed. "That is a very involved subject—too lengthy for this afternoon," one minister replied. "Actually, I just have time to get to another appointment." He seemed in a hurry.

Then the other two pastors also found that they had appointments too. All three rose to leave. Then, one of them turned back and whispered, "Sister Nelson, you just do what you think is right."

That encounter convinced the deliberate and careful Gustava about the validity of the seventh-day Sabbath. Without further ado the Nelson family themselves became "Advents." The whole family along with many other Sabbath-keepers went to church on the streetcar. After fighting the decision for ten years, Anders Nelson was baptized on Easter Sabbath, 1907. That same day Gustava joined by profession of faith.

How the threads of so many lives had been woven together! It all began when Anders Nelson jumped aboard that ship bound for America. What if he'd missed that step? Well, that, to be sure, would have been an altogether different story. At last, he began to comprehend that destiny into which he had leaped that day.

[1] At different times Castle Garden served as a theater, an opera house, and an aquarium. Today it is Castle Clinton National Monument, the ticket center for ferries to Ellis Island and the Statue of Liberty. During its time as an Immigration Center eight million people came through its doors (1855-1892).

[2] The Nelsons were Danish for only one day, July 4, 1886 Thereafter, the census listings in Washington state (1910, 1920, 1930) regularly listed them as Swedish.

[3] Anders Nelson had fulfilled the five-year waiting period and had become a U. S. citizen. The day Gustava married him she too acquired citizenship.

[4] The Nelson's second baby, Edith, was stillborn.

4. The Way Up and Out

One day Gustava wondered what Andrew and Philip might be doing in the basement. She called downstairs, "What are you doing, Andrew?"

"Nothing." All parents, of course, have learned to be wary of this standard explanation coming from their busy but silent children.

"What are *you* doing, Philip?" Suspicious, Gustava pressed her point.

"Helping Andrew, Mama," piped a cheerful little voice.

With typical enterprise Andrew N. got a job delivering papers to the homes on the hill behind their home. Later he developed a profitable paper-route downtown. At about this same time the whole city was excited when the first airplane came to Seattle. All of the Nelsons took the streetcar down town to see the wonderful flying machine come in over Elliot Bay. Then, with the skills of a real entrepreneur, young Andrew entered a contest sponsored by the Seattle newspaper. His model plane won third prize in its class.

On December 5, 1907, Andrew and Gustava welcomed their last baby. That day the other children spent the afternoon and evening at the Sletigrens house next door. After a good dinner, the young Nelsons went home to find that they had a new baby sister. Delighted, Reuben raced around the house yelling, "I'm not the baby any more."

His older brother Andrew, however, had just figured out the full implications of the event. Now he knew why Mama hadn't been feeling too well and why *he* had been the one doing the laundry for several weeks.

He looked down at the baby. "She is very sweet, Mama. But," he added diplomatically, "let's not have any more!"

Although she was named Olivia after the dear Mrs. Sletigren, Gustava took to calling her *Vannen* (Sw. "little friend"). Thus, the little girl grew up to be "Vivian."

Two years later, the Nelsons moved for the last time. With great care, Andrew chose a very large, pleasant lot. He built their "dream house" at 1208 Shelby Street" on Lake Union. This glacial, freshwater lake lay entirely within the city limits of Seattle, and a ship channel connected it with the sea in Puget Sound.

The dining-room doorway looked across to Lake Washington and the Cascade Mountains. The two huge windows opened out on Lake Union where big freighters signaled the bridges to open for them and where small craft scurried to and fro nearby.

The kitchen had plenty of cupboards, two cooking ranges and a special table for Gustava to knead her bread. Its windows opened onto the garden. The large, railed-in back porch not only commanded a great view of Lake Washington and Lake Union, but was the favorite entryway into the house. There were three large tubs for Gustava's scrubbing, boiling, and rinsing clothes on washday. It also harbored generations of cats and dogs.

Two bedrooms and a bath downstairs and more bedrooms upstairs gave everyone space. Prominently displayed over the fireplace hung a formal portrait of *Kung au Sverige* (the "King of Sweden"). While the Nelson children grew up in a generation that considered things Swedish to be old fashioned and low class, Andrew and Gustava always loved their homeland. After many years, Mama Nelson finally moved the king from the living room to the upstairs landing. "We're American now," she announced briefly. Although she didn't particularly care for her name, Gustava was fully aware of its royal lineage. For the latter part of her lifetime, King Gustav V (1907-1950) of ancient descent, sat on the throne in her homeland.

Once in a while, with perhaps a faint touch of defiance, Gustava would look around her comfortable home and remember the cutting remark of her long-ago mistress in Helsingborg: "You're a *piga*, and you'll always be a *piga*!" Maybe, even back then she'd known that the insult could not—would not—be true.

Still, Sweden remained close to the heart of the family. Papa Nelson always said his blessings and prayers in Swedish. When he went off to college, Andrew N. studied Swedish as a minor at Walla Walla.

Right after the family settled in at 1208, their front yard provided a prime viewpoint for seeing the fireworks of the 1908 Alaska-Yukon-

Pacific Exposition. For more tangible entertainment, the children had a series of rafts tied up at their dock, and they never tired of water games. Their rowboat was named "Vivian" for the youngest, supposedly to prevent competition among the older children. That little skipper learned to row almost automatically. The little girl was barely four years old when Gustava looked out of the window one day to see her out in the middle of the lake, rowing like a professional.

Christmas at 1208 held enduring memories. After a delicious supper at the big dining room table, Papa sat in a large, bent-wood rocker, under the big portrait of his Mother Kama that looked down solemnly on them all. Mama sat by the tree on the other side. In between, the children sat in a semi-circle. The conversation went around the circle while everyone told the others what they were thankful for. Vivian recalled "the wonder of the fire, the unusual warmth, the magic of the tree." It was a time for "being together again after the older children had been away to college." The presents were predictable and commonplace enough but given with love— underwear, new stockings, shoe polish, shoelaces, hairpins, and the like. Mama always made a new nightshirt for each of her men-folk. Then a special treat–like an orange or a can of pineapple–might top it all off.

By the time he was in his teens, Andrew had learned the meaning of work and the beauty of compassion. He chopped wood, worked in the garden, mowed the lawn and picked wild blackberries. All useful to his family's well-being. The Nelson children had games to play, but perhaps swimming in the beautiful lake that looked across to the city of Seattle was their favorite pastime.

One day in the city Andrew found a homeless man who had lost one arm. "Please, can you give me a dime. I'm hungry." Andrew promptly gave him the only dime he had and went without lunch himself that day.

Andrew graduated from Broadway High School the year that the family moved to 1208 Shelby Street. He still wondered why only Seventh-day Adventists kept the seventh-day. His parents sent the eighteen-year-old off to Walla Walla College. "Go there and study it out for yourself, son," his father advised.

When his classmates suggested that maybe he was actually going to the Walla Walla State Penitentiary, Andrew was not in the least amused. In his first letter home he wrote: "The only thing that keeps me here is that I don't have the train fare to get home!"

Soon, however, his letters became shorter and happier. His parents were much pleased to learn that he was baptized in the middle of his freshman year at Walla Walla. He had been much influenced by his roommate, Joe Hall.

That summer (1911) he wrote home to announce that he was bringing four of his college friends with him. Joe Hall was recovering from a difficult tonsillectomy and could not go to his home. Three more[1] just wanted to come with him. They'd be staying at 1208 only from Friday to Monday morning. The rest of the week they'd be out canvassing to earn their college tuition for the next school year. "We have room in the big house, Mama, and we'll all help with the work." At first, Gustava probably didn't realize that she'd be baking nine loaves of bread three times a week!

Young Nelson always knew where he wanted to go, even if he wasn't always sure how to get there. That first summer he got lost in the woods searching for the home of a Mr. Green. Asking a few directions along the way, he rushed down the woodland trail, as he described it, "hopping logs and dodging trees" until he found the bachelor's cabin.

It was only 8:00 p.m. but the householder was already in bed. Bent on business, Andrew knocked on the door. "I'm far into the woods, and I'm not sure where I am. I need help finding my way out."

"Wow!" Green replied. "Would you like to come in and sleep in my house tonight?"

"That would suit me fine," young Andrew replied. The two sat in the dark and talked for a while. An hour later, they went to bed— and then talked another hour beyond that. The discussion resumed at breakfast in the morning. Andrew later recalled talking about the current strikes in England. Then he seized upon his chance. "That's exactly what my book deals with," Andrew exclaimed. Forthwith, he sold Mr. Green the book right there on the doorstep.

Through the summer's canvassing he was frequently offered meals and a place to sleep. Sometimes sales worked. Sometimes not. "The devil tries to discourage me, but he can't," Andrew wrote. "Some people think that I am just out to make money and tell me I ought to be ashamed of myself to try to make money on such a scheme." Always he persuaded himself to "cheerily go on." Eyes fixed on the prize, he'd already discovered many kinds of rewards. Book selling, in fact, would see Andrew all the way through to his bachelor's degree in 1915.

Andrew's first educational ambition had been to join the U. S. Government Geological Survey and work out on the high Pacific shore at Puget Sound. God had other plans,[2] and in his sophomore year at Walla Walla College he chose subjects that forecast his future interests: library science, education, pastoral training, Greek and literature. He also taught classes to the 8th and 9th graders.

He augmented his physics studies with a profound interest in astronomy. In fact, he occasionally gave talks on the subject. "I was greatly enamored," he wrote, "over the prospects which we have before us in the company of Jesus in the New Earth and off into space. Don't you think we'll make inter-stellar voyages? I do, as I watch those faraway worlds. The stars that so crisply twinkled in the cool of the night get my attention so I can hardly leave them. Watching month after month and year after year, we see them shift. Whither they are all going, we know not, for they're so far away. Yet we see them."

College life and teaching kept Andrew so busy that he could really appreciate Sabbath. "I am glad that Sabbath does come around every seven days, otherwise I'd soon go up in smoke."

He and his roommates, Guy and Joe, sometimes had their "room-work" done by 2:50 p.m. This included haircut, shave, and a bath. Also pressed clothes. "Marvelous occurrence!" Andrew chortled.

After graduation in 1915, Andrew Nelson stepped into his first job. He became principal of the ten-grade church school at Oriens, in Seattle. At the same time, he taught all of the 9th and 10th-grade subjects. Although he felt fortunate to have the job, he soon realized that the load was "killing" him. His innate gifts for leadership sprang into the foreground at this point.

He decided that he had to manage his time better. Each evening he carefully organized all of the necessary activities for the next day. He also decreed that he would not say anything about others that he would not want to be said about himself. Thus, with God's help, he accomplished even more than he imagined. At the end of the school year he was able to define certain mileposts:

1. Students were more successful in their studies.
2. Discipline was under control.
3. Improvements had been made to the school plant.
4. A strong library had been established.
5. Spiritual growth had been seen among both staff and students.

Herein lay the roots of the natural educator that Andrew Nelson was yet to become.

Meanwhile, with World War I in full force, Andrew knew that the Draft Board was looking for him. He appealed for an exemption but was philosophical about the prospects. He was not going to escape as his father had done a generation earlier. While friends and family prayed for him to avoid being drafted, he knew that God would keep him "true," no matter which way the decision went. (His freedom from military service was not finally insured until March, 1918.)

In the midst of this uncertainty, young Andrew got a new job with the Western Washington Conference of Seventh-day Adventists. He left his teaching job in Seattle to assist Pastor S. N. Rittenhouse in the new district of Winlock.[3]

Later, that same year, an event of cosmic significance occurred at camp meeting time. It began very early on a Sabbath morning when he went into the main tent. No one was there except one girl, sitting by herself. For perhaps the only time in his life, Andrew heard a voice: "That is the girl you are going to marry."

Maybe the clarity of this message accounts for Andrew's uncharacteristic ineptitude a few days earlier. His sister Gertrude had come over from Seattle to help him set up his personal tent. They divided it neatly into a sitting-dining room and two bedrooms. Gertrude was determined to make theirs the most attractive lodging in all of the long rows of tents.

All that remained was to level off a sandbox for the base of their stove. Andrew had a little trouble. "Just hold the box straight," he told his sister, "so the kettle doesn't overflow. I'll be back to fix it in just a few minutes."

Gertrude waited. And waited. She still had to make the beds, she thought impatiently. Where had Andrew gone? He was never this irresponsible.

Finally he showed up. No excuse or apology. "Oh, Gert!" he cried. "I've just met the most beautiful young lady I've ever seen!" He went on to explain that Vera Shoff had just graduated from the nursing course at Portland Sanitarium and was thinking of enrolling at Walla Walla College.

Over the next several days Andrew met Vera's mother and her two aunts. As a conference employee it was, naturally, his duty to convince them all that Walla Walla was a fine Christian college and that Vera should go there. This concern occupied a good deal of his attention. Indeed, thoughts of Vera swept his memory clean of any of the other girls he'd ever met. She was, in fact, the girl he'd seen sitting alone in the big tent.

After camp meeting Andrew was engaged in searching for a new site for a new church-sponsored high school. The Seattle-Tacoma area, midway between the Cascade Mountains and Puget Sound, seemed a good option. A property in the small town of Auburn seemed to fill the bill. Andrew found that a ticket on the inter-urban streetcar from Seattle to Auburn was cheaper if you bought a ticket to Kent (where Vera lived) and then purchased another one from Kent to Auburn. He felt this to be an important discovery and certainly a money-saving device for his employers.

In actual fact, Vera did enroll at the College, but she stayed for just one semester. Love had overtaken both her and Andrew.

Andrew's career now evolved at astonishing speed. He had barely joined the ministerial work force when his appointment changed. Next he served as Educational, Y. P. (Young People), & S. S. (Sabbath School) Secretary" in the Western Washington Conference. A small conference, to be sure, but twenty-four-year-old Andrew became one of its five administrative officers.[4]

Immediately he visited all sixty churches and church schools in his district. He found that only sixteen of the schools were offering daily instruction in the Bible, the "Book of Wisdom' he highly recommended. Still, he wrote an upbeat report, full of ideas that would work themselves out fully in the school leadership roles that he would fulfill in future years.[5]

His itinerant school visits appear to have covered a creative range of topics. A reporter at Meadow Glade Academy, Seattle, wrote of "Professor Nelson's" enjoyable visit. On March 16 and 17, 1918, "several very interesting meetings were held." In this context, the title of "professor" for the very youthful church administrator is surprising. In some way, Andrew Nelson already bore the marks of the scholarly achievement that would distinguish his later career.

Meanwhile, Andrew would have read the *Gleaner's* pre-Christmas issue of December 18, 1917. As an experienced colporteur, he would have noted two items of interest. B. P. Hoffman's essay, "Literature Work in Japan," described the first Adventist book in Japan, *Owari no Fukuin* ("The Gospel for the Last Days") that had been published back in 1898. Now the Japanese Mission was printing *Toki no Shirushi* ("Signs of the Times"), a thirty-two-page magazine. The church had paid 1,000 yen for a license allowing them to discuss current events. This privilege, of course, was essential to the presentation of Biblical prophecy. The article was followed by a list of available books and tracts in the Japanese language. The *Gleaner* appealed to readers to supply the "foreign field at your very doors." That is, "the thousands of Japanese in the western [United] States."[6]

Another forecast of the future for Andrew appears in the report that he had, with "personal effort" contacted about fifty of our (Seventh-day Adventist) boys at Camp Lewis. Already he had the instincts of a military chaplain. A week later, Pastor Rittenhouse announced that a "baby church" had been founded in Winlock—the first district to which Andrew had been assigned. Happily, the twenty new members were "working hard," having distinguished themselves at Harvest Ingathering.[7]

Although Nelson now had no part in the Winlock enterprise he would still experience the hard times of "frontier evangelism." Ever ready for the task at hand, Andrew, along with L. E. Tupper, began an evangelistic campaign in Kelso, Washington. Since the local Baptist congregation had no pastor, they cheerfully rented their church to the Adventists. The average attendance, however, decreased markedly when a disgruntled member forced the Adventists to leave the church and rent a public hall.

The two men analyzed their rather disappointing results. They had to, because, in general, church papers called for accountability. That meant numbers!! They identified three detriments to their work: The deception of socialism, the influence of some "Holy Rollers" (from the previous summer), along with very severe weather and much illness. Finally, they could account for just three "sure" interests and a "fair" attendance. Still, a final optimistic note (probably written by Andrew) declared: "Our Sabbath School is growing, and we have organized a Junior Young People's Society."[8] In February, 1918, optimism came easily to Andrew.

He and the lovely Vera married on March 24, 1918. For their honeymoon they attended the General Conference session in San Francisco.

Meanwhile at home a crisis had arisen. The day after the wedding in Kent the Nelsons arrived home at 1208 St. very late. The next morning ten-year-old Vivian assumed that she wouldn't have to go to school because Andrew and Vera were on their honeymoon. Mama Nelson combed the tangles out of her hair. "Mama, you're killing me," the disappointed child cried.

The always-capable Gustava didn't miss a stroke. "No, *Vannen*," she replied. "It isn't *that* easy to die."

Actually, Gustava became violently ill during the day. The little confrontation that morning had cost more endurance than even she had. She very nearly died, but was back on duty soon after Andrew and Vera returned to their tiny two-room house in Auburn, Washington.

One delightful surprise Andrew made about Vera was her great knowledge of managing a home. Along with her nursing studies, she'd become an excellent cook and mistress of all household arts.

Together the bride and groom watched a solar eclipse and the "brief, creepy night" that it caused. "The corona was a beautiful sight," Andrew recorded in his diary. "It was not the darkness of night, nor extreme darkness of the dark day of 1780. . . .We could easily see each other and the buildings. Near the end of the two or three minute period, I noticed sunset colors in the west—red and silver. But I [kept] my eyes on the corona. The western light brightened! And as suddenly as before, a little speck of the sun dazzled forth, and daylight was there again, to remain [for another] 100 years."

The newlyweds didn't know it yet, but their links with their homeland were about to loosen—permanently. By the next Christmas they would be living and working in Japan.

---

[1] Andrew Nelson's other friends were Walter Consuylman, Guy Joergenson, and James Hoskihara.
[2] *Far Eastern Division Outlook* (September, 1936), p. 4.
[3] *North Pacific Union Gleaner,* Vol. 12, No. 13 (July 25, 1917).
[4] *North Pacific Union Gleaner,* Vol. 12, No. 17 (August 23, 1917), p. 5.
[5] *North Pacific Union Gleaner,* Vol. 12, No. 20 (September 13, 1917), p.11; Vol. 12, No.22 (September 27, 1917), p. 3.
[6] *North Pacific Union Gleaner,* Vol. 12, No. 33 (December 18, 1917), p. 3.
[7] *North Pacific Union Gleaner,* Vol. 12, No. 27 (November 1, 1917), p. 3; Vol. 12, No. 28 (November 8, 1917), p. 3.
[8] *North Pacific Union Gleaner,* Vol. 12, No. 33 (January 3, 1918), p. 2; Vol. 12, No. 40 (February 7, 1918), p. 1.

Roots In Sweden

1. Anders/Andrew A. Nelson (1865-1948). He sent this picture from Helena, Territory of Montana, about 1888. He wanted Gustava to remember who he was while he worked to learn English and establish himself as a wage-earning builder.

2. Gustava Caroline Jonson (1866-1930), the "Beautiful Girl on the Ship." This was the first picture Anders had of her. He never forgot.

3. Anders' very capable mother, Kama Swanstrom, kept two servant girls, ran the water-powered mill, and kept a bakery in town.

4.

4. Family historian, Vivian Nelson-Cushman, stands with her cousins in front of the family home in Janstrop, Sweden, where Anders Nelson was born in 1865.

5. Another view of the original family home.

5.

6.

6. The old kyrka dominates the village of Byrnakulla, Sweden, where Gustava Jonson was born in 1866.

7. Upon reaching America, Gustava (left) was reunited with her very dear friend Moster **Emma in Kansas City, Missouri.**

8. Unfailing loyalty to her homeland sometimes persuaded Gustava to pose for a picture in Swedish dress.

9. Anders Nelson and Gustava Jonson sat for their first portrait together in Kansas City in 1891. It served as their engagement-and-wedding picture, all in one.

The Andrew A. Nelson Family

10. In Seattle, 1905. At the back a very young teenager, Andrew Nathaniel Nelson, stood between his parents Andrew and Gustava Nelson. Reuben sat at the left and Philip stood at the right. Gertrude sat center-front, tending her doll, Margaret, in the doll carriage. This favorite family photograph always had a place of honor in the house. Vivian, the youngest, was always disappointed that she was born two years too late to be in it.

11.

11. Firstborn, Andrew, stood for his first portrait in Great Falls, Montana. Enveloped in the elegantly formal clothes of the time, he wore boots and a skirt concurrently.

12. From the start, Andrew took his little sister Gertrude in hand.

12.

13. When her third son, Reuben, was born in 1901, Mama Gustava went for a studio portrait.

13.

14. Baby Vivian and her brother Reuben could not persuade the cat to stay in the picture.

15. Later on, the dog elected to pose with Vivian and Philip.

16. When thirteen-year-old Vivian graduated from Grade 8, she wanted to stand with her teacher, Big Sister Gertrude.

17. & 18. At one time or another all of the young Nelsons went off to Walla Walla College, Washington. Left, Philip. Right, Vivian.

19. With his well-honed building skills, Andrew A. Nelson never failed to keep his family well-housed. The first one was at 914 8th Avenue North in Great Falls, in the Montana Territory. The first son, Andrew N., was born here.

20. Papa Andrew built a second—better—house two streets over, at 142 6th Avenue North, Great Falls.

21. This house on 2337 North Broadway, Seattle, set the Nelson family next door to the Sletingrens who were Seventh-day Adventists. A significant connection.

Our beloved + happy home.

22. The final "dream home" on Lake Union, Seattle, was at 1208 Shelby Street. From that point on, the Nelsons simply labeled themselves the 1208 Family.

23. Papa Andrew A. Nelson, a widower for seventeen years, sold the beloved "1208" home in Seattle (in 1945) and moved to Southern California. This is the last, formal picture of the stalwart man who long ago took that leap into a great destiny and never turned back.

23.

24.

24. When Anders and Gustava left Sweden in 1886, Oscar II was the King of Sweden. For many years they proudly displayed a large picture of him in their home. Finally, at 1208 Shelby Street, Gustava removed the portrait from its place of honor over the living room fireplace and hung it on the upstairs landing. "We're Americans now," she explained.

The Andrew N. Nelson Family

25. & 26. Wedding portraits. Andrew N. Nelson and Vera Shoff married on
March 24, 1918, in Kent Washington.

27. A solemn family on the Seattle dock, as Andrew and Vera
Nelson wait to sail for Japan (1918).

28.

JAPAN

28. When the Nelsons said their good-byes to Andrew and Vera in 1918, they stood for all of the families who have given their children up to foreign mission service.

29.

29. In Seattle, 1918. Front, L to R: Papa Andrew Nelson, Vivian, Mama Gustava. Back, L to R: Reuben, Andrew, Vera, Gertrude, Philip.

30. Andrew N. Nelson had begun to look quite professorial by the time he took up his work in Tokyo.

31. As Andrew and Vera Nelson embraced the Japanese language and culture, they also learned to enjoy the comfort of wearing silk kimonos.

32. Andrew and Vera enjoyed Richard, their 2 ½ month-old firstborn, in Tokyo (1920).

33. For his second birthday (March 2, 1922), Richard received a wicker rocking chair.

34. Aboard ship en route home to Seattle, Vera (right) was happy when a fellow passenger lent an extra pair of hands to help with her three little ones.

35. While the Nelsons went to Japan as newly-weds (1918), on their first furlough (1923) they came home with three children: Richard and the twins Dorothy and Donald.

36. & 37. Family portraits for the Andrew Nelson family took on a regular pattern: Richard standing between the twins.

38. By 1927, Donald (right) has gained a slight edge in height over his twin sister Dorothy (left).

39. The Andrew Nelson Family portrait. (1933)

5. Off to Japan

In the summer of 1918, Andrew and Vera Nelson took the train down to San Francisco to attend the quadrennial session of the General Conference of Seventh-day Adventists. In fact, this constituted their honeymoon trip.

Not surprisingly this striking young couple found themselves recruited into foreign mission service. They met B. P. Hoffmann, superintendent of the Japan Mission and author of the report on Christian book publishing that they'd read just a few months earlier. Even more importantly, they met Elder W. A. Spicer who had already attained international fame as a writer and educator. After they had lunch with him one day, the winds of change almost blew them off their feet.

By the end of the meetings the couple had an official invitation to work in Japan. That island chain, more than 2,000 miles long, would become their new workplace. The Nelsons never looked back. For them, it was "all systems go." Returning home, they packed up their little house and moved to the little dairy-farming town of Kent, Washington, where they spent their last weeks with Vera's parents.

From there Andrew went back south to Auburn to tie up the loose ends of his work in the Western Washington Conference office. Their last bit of service was given in July when they took part in an evangelistic campaign in Renton (twelve miles southeast of Seattle). Both Andrew and Vera were there for the tent pitching, in heavy rain. Although opposition in the strongly Roman Catholic town ran high, the report ended on a high note. All five workers claimed to be "of good courage."[1]

Then in August 1918 they sailed from Seattle on the *Kamu Maru*. During the long voyage they invested hours in watching the antics of the porpoises, seagulls, and flying fish. That month spent steaming across the Pacific spared the Nelsons the stress of jet-lag and also gave them ample time to become acquainted with fellow passengers. They spent more hours on deck just staring into the indigo blue waves with white curls of foam rolling continually back over them. Then again they would retreat to their cabin for their own worship times when they could plead with God to give them special guidance in their new work in Japan.

Finally, the *Kamu Maru* docked in Yokohama on October 2, 1918. A group of Adventist workers, both foreign and national, met the ship and took the new missionaries to the compound at Ogikubo, a suburb of Tokyo.

The Nelsons found their new home in Tokyo delightful. Already the Amanuma compound had been voted the most lovely mission site in the Orient. The setting immediately appealed to the astronomer in Andrew. He wrote: "The church is a prettily located one at the corner of the compound, painted a nice blue color and topped by a neat steeple. At the full noon she is especially beautiful as the orb of night shines from the east upon her. I love to linger near her shadows on those evenings."

Not only did the General Conference President, I. H. Evans, praise this attractive mission compound in Tokyo, he also liked Andrew on sight: "Everyone who knows Brother Nelson expects great things of him," he reported.[2]

By this time, on the home front, Andrew Nelson had found utter joy in "sweet Vera, the nurse." He described her cooking as "exquisite." Some weeks later he wrote: "I think of the girl whom I chose as a companion in making a home. [Our marriage] is a great success and a happy home is assured. . . . In every way Vera has been a help, and now we have successfully weathered a winter and are out of debt, the thing that so many think is a necessary adjunct to married life. . . .Our resources (besides a complete supply of personal effects and bedroom and kitchen furniture) has turned out to be one yen!"

As the capital of the Empire, Tokyo was replete with the Imperial Palace, parliament and foreign embassies. In contrast to the American Northwest the Nelsons had left behind them, the city was listed as the most densely populated spot on earth, in proportion to its size. Little by little, they came to realize that they'd arrived in beautiful Japan in "hard times." On the one hand, the Japanese were "intelligent, reading people" and they actually had money. (One of missionaries on a Japanese train one day observed that out of the twenty passengers in his car seventeen were reading books and magazines.)

The country was, however, at war with China and the huge rise in the cost of living had caused "rice riots." Also, unusually severe storms and floods had ravaged the countryside. Additionally, several Adventist missionaries had returned home for health reasons or had been on extended furloughs.[3]

The hard times notwithstanding, Andrew Nelson had arrived, as it turned out, on the very "cusp of opportunity." He and Vera were immediately sent to intensive language study at Tokyo's Language School.[4] Andrew's linguistic skills became obvious in the first year.

Indeed, his talents matched a decision that the Church had been overdue in making. Administrators finally decided that language study was essential to evangelistic success. When W. C. Grainger first brought Adventism to Japan in 1896, missionaries made little effort to learn the Japanese language. The main contacts between the two groups occurred when people came to the mission to learn English.

With their first year of language study now behind them, the Nelsons attended the third annual meeting of the Japan Conference, held at Gotemba, a mountain resort near Mt. Fuji (August 18-23, 1919).[5] Since the islands of Japan were strung out over such a great distance, just getting delegates together for a general meeting had been a task in itself.

Then a typhoon struck on the first day, delaying the arrival of some travelers. The storm however, didn't prevent the transaction of two important pieces of business.

First, Japan was voted into a "Union Mission" comprised of six local missions each with its own director. Of the six, three had Japanese leaders with no foreign assistance.[6] Heavy emphasis was placed on education, so these important organizational changes had to be made. Andrew Nelson was given the management of the southernmost, Kyushu.

Although the membership statistics for Japan were dismaying (a total of about 300), the spirit of the meeting was reportedly excellent. The six new directors were admonished: "[Now you] have every opportunity to demonstrate [your] ability in soul-winning work." To this end Andrew Nelson and Perry Webber were ordained to the gospel ministry. Probably more than once Andrew contemplated the challenge ahead of him and recalled his previous evangelistic endeavors in Seattle as being rather mild in contrast. Less than fifty Adventists lived in his whole district.

W. A. Spicer was a General Conference visitor at the gathering.

A notable Church educator, he had bemoaned the fact that "We have moved [so] slowly in Japan." Still, he had been thrilled to watch the interchange between the foreign workers and the Japanese, all speaking, "in the vernacular." He noted that Elder Hoffmann, the mission superintendent, "had a reading and speaking knowledge of the Japanese language" and that he was popular with the local people. An obvious asset to be developed!

Spicer had already decided the language study had to take a front seat, especially in a country like Japan whose language "wields so much influence in the Far East." Perhaps more than anyone else in Church administration, he grasped these vital insights. At the same time, he hastened to subdue potential anxieties. "These Oriental tongues need in no wise terrify our youth who are willing to work hard."

Indeed, Adventist missionaries seemed to be acquiring language efficiency in amazingly short periods of time. He pointed out, young Andrew Nelson of Walla Walla as a case in point. At the end of this first year of language study he had been chosen to receive the diplomas from the Japanese Minister of Education and hand them out to his class in the Tokyo Language School. A class made up largely of missionaries of "all societies."[7]

Meanwhile, Vera's professional skills had quickly been recognized and called into service. When both of the Hoffmanns fell ill with the flu, they sent for Vera. She presently nursed them both back to health. Andrew anxiously cautioned his young wife to be careful, but then he had to tell himself that she had "a strong resistance to germs anyway." Lonely, during her absence, he took serious time just to think about and to appreciate the girl he'd married.

Upon entering into his duties as one of the new mission directors, Andrew Nelson requested that he be allowed a second year of language study. He knew he needed it.

One rainy night he visited a nearby farmhouse. "Although I had a good time, the language is really a barrier. When will I ever get to the place where I can speak freely? The young man was interested in my God, bless him. I am now teaching English, which is much easier than speaking Japanese."

It was, of course, still much too early to understand where Andrew's zeal for the Japanese language would take him. The day would come when he would be completely "free" with the Japanese language.

[1] *North Pacific Union Gleaner,* Vol. 13, No 13 (August 1, 1918), p. 4.

[2] I. H. Evans, "A Month in Japan," *Review & Herald* (September 4, 1919), pp. 15-16.

[3] B. P. Hoffman, "Japan" *Review & Herald* (April 10, 1919), pp. 20-21; *Asiatic Division Outlook* (February 1, 1919), p. 3.

[4] *Review & Herald* (April 10, 1919), pp.20-21. Fresh back from his furlough and attending the General Conference Session, President Hoffman reported the arrival of the Nelsons. See *Asiatic Division Outlook* (February 1, 1918), p. 3.

[5] *Review & Herald* (November 13, 1919).

[6] The six divisions of the Japanese Mission Union voted in August, 1919:

> 1. S. G. Jacques, Hokkaido, the northernmost island (population 2½ million).
> 2. H. F. Benson, Aizu Wakamatsu, northern portion of the main island. (population 8 million). A mission home and small church had been built.
> 3. H. Kunyiya, Tokyo, north central portion ot the main island (population 16 million). Meetings had to be held in a single room in a private home.
> 4. Brother Okohira. Kansi Mission, including Kobe and Nagoya (population 10 million).
> 5. Brother Kobayashi. Chugoku Mission, including Hiroshima (population 8 million).
> 6. Andrew Nelson. Kyushu, southern island.

[7] W. A. Spicer, "The Message in Japan," *Review & Herald* (December 18, 1919), p. 5. In the language school in China Leroy E. Froom held second place in studies in the Manderin language. Right behind him were the Harold Grahams, an Adventist couple from Mount Vernon Academy.

6. On Task

Andrew Nelson's early days in Japan entranced him. He called the country "a delightful land where life was safe and sane and happy." The people exhibited many "surprising virtues," such as "honesty, industry, cleanliness, precision, kindness, democracy, and courtesy." Moreover, those pleasant days "were marked by cordial Japan-American relations." Above all, Japan enjoyed "freedom to think, talk, and worship."

Nelson's personal energy knew no bounds. In the midst of his language-learning efforts, he undertook some canvassing. "In one day I sold two books and six magazines." He confessed to the difficulty of making the sales in Japanese: My limitations soon made me run out of selling points."

After this experiment he wisely turned over the canvassing and home missionary work to his assistant, Ogura San. Along with Perry Webber, Andrew managed the little training school in Tokyo. What had begun in 1914 as the "Japan School of Evangelism" was called *Amanuma Gakuin* in 1919.

"Busy to the breaking point," he taught classes in English, Japanese, and New Testament History. At the same time, he did bookkeeping for the Mission and served as elder of the Amanuma church. He knew he'd never worked harder in his life.

Often frustrated at the language barrier he would sometimes say, "When will I *ever* get to the place where I can speak freely?" Finally, at the end of his second year of language study, he felt that he'd "passed the critical stage. . . . [And] with God's help I can soon have a good command of this, my third native tongue, the Nipponese."

Meanwhile, his inquiring mind processed every potential avenue to self-improvement. Always tuned in to the fine points of language he formulated his own theory on speech.

My Theory of How to Talk

1. Be silent, if speaking is unnecessary.
2. When you have something to say, say it.
3. Prepare a very clear outline.
4. Aim to teach a specific point.
5. Use many very interesting illustrations.
6. Know what you're talking about.
7. Don't use words out of place for emphasis
8. Words have a definite meaning and should be used definitely.

In due course, fatherhood brought new ideas into Andrew's already vigorous life. His first child, Richard, was born on March 2, 1920. By the time the baby was seven months old his father was virtually crowing with delight. "[Little Richard is] a real pleasure for us. His smile is angelic! To watch it sparkle in the eyes first and then form upon the lips is indeed a glimpse of heaven. Our darling baby is getting cuter every day. We have just bought a large play basket for him."

That same year Andrew took the first steps into what would become a lifelong commitment to education. The Japan Mission Training School had opened in Tokyo on October 1, 1919. Early reports courageously recorded that more than forty bright young people were enrolled. Some of them worked in the mission offices and others translated books into Japanese. (These "books" were distributed in mimeograph form.) Although still attending the Tokyo Language School, Andrew taught three English classes at the infant school.[1]

About this same time Andrew mapped out an entire master plan for living. In his usual rational way of thinking, he admitted that he'd "made many mistakes in Japan" but rejoiced that he'd "mended them all." He'd accepted criticism and built upon it. Maintaining that, "nearly all criticism has a grain of truth," he collected all of those grains and removed them. The result? Criticism became groundless and, in fact, almost ceased. This line of self-examination led him to produce his own credo.

Andrew Nelson's Master Plan for Living (1920)

I have learned that:

1. I must pay for my own board and room, 365 days a year.
2. It is best to follow the conventions of society.
3. I must not concern myself with the personal affairs of another.
4. It does no good to appear "put out" about anything.
5. I must weigh evidence and judge and decide for myself. I must gather complete wisdom, think carefully, and conclude independently.
6. I must not change when I know the correct reasoning.
7. I should decide quickly. As a rule, it is best to decide a thing now and save time.
8. Whenever you or the other fellow is heated, the less said the better.
9. Hosts of unpleasant matters can be disposed of by simply forgetting.
10. When I ask subordinates to do a thing, [I should] expect them to get it done, forgetting myself.
11. In doing many things in a short time, I must become efficient and not waste nerve energy.
12. When I have wronged others, I must make it right at the first opportunity. Then the past is past, and my only concerns are the present and future.
13. I must distrust and hate flattery. I must be able to judge commendation and to take it aright.
14. My past has been a rush, interspersed with periods of lethargy and laziness. I must cease procrastination and be more even and steady in my work.
15. I have learned much about efficiency and leadership lately– and I must learn more.
16. I must not reveal the skeleton of my plans but present them clothed in flesh.
17. It is not always best to be too brief in stating a conclusion, if you do not have listeners with you.
18. When I discover a good thing, I should stay with it regardless of what others may think about it.
19. Thinking about business on Sabbath dries up my spirituality.
20. Though habit is strong, with tremendous effort I can break any habit.
21. Heart politeness is a most happy possession.

Two years later, Vera was pregnant again. A girl, or another boy? It turned out to be both. A nurse at St. Luke's hospital declared that the patient was carrying twins. The doctor replied somewhat haughtily. "I can't find a second heartbeat, so it must be a single birth." On the evening of October 31, 1922, Vera went into labor and delivered a son, just before midnight. The "next day" (November 1) at 1:30 a.m. a sturdy girl appeared. She contradicted the doctor, affirmed the nurse, and totally surprised the parents. They named the twins Donald and Dorothy.

After two more years of family life Andrew Nelson prepared his "Notebook Resolutions," a kind of addendum to his "Master-plan" of 1920. "It is," he explained, "very concrete and very practical, resulting from my love of playing with system. On one side of my notebook is my time, systematically planned. On the other side are my money budgets and accounts. It relieves me of all minor matters and leaves my mind free for remembering important matters." Although $33 might appear to have been a good salary at the time, with a family of five, Andrew found it difficult "to keep well" on that income.

Now, at thirty years of age, he realized that he still had much to learn. On the other hand, he—with justification—had crowded in a lot of experience and could recall "no wasted time."

The Notebook Resolutions
(1924)
The Aims

1. I resolve to make my own home one where harsh speech will not be heard.
2. I make a lot of mistakes (I suppose everyone does), but I find wonderful comfort if I can capture one lesson out of each mistake and this I usually manage to do.
3. I must not court flattery nor give any opportunity to people to flatter me.
4. I have overcome strange thinking (laziness) and can now tussle with difficult problems of any kind.
5. I have, from the bottom of my heart, cancelled bluffing, haphazardness, and lack of system.
6. I have a speed problem. I have developed a high speed in thinking and working that borders on nervousness. I am now beginning to cut this speed down to a safe limit.
7. I have learned to relax, both physically and mentally.

Andrew Nelson elaborated frequently on God's systematic universe. He looked forward to the time when God would finally "give the signal" and halt all of this world's activities with Christ's Second Coming. He studied the millennium in heaven, the judgment, the punishment of the wicked, the New Earth, our "luxurious, and beautiful home" in the Holy City, and inter-galactic travel. Everything revealed a perfect sequence in God's sense of system. Personally, he found it simply "second nature" to comply with all of God's requirements for salvation.

Along the way, through morning and evening family worship, he and Vera had instilled the same kind of self-discipline in their three little ones.

One day, as Mother sat in the living room she noticed Richard in the adjacent dining room, eying the delicious basket of fruit on the table. Despite the prevailing household law about not eating between meals, he reached for an apple. After a moment's hesitation, he returned it to the basket. Failing to leave the scene of temptation, however, he picked it up again.

On the third time, he was about to take a bite out of it. "No," the little fellow suddenly cried, dropping the apple back into the basket. "No, Satan! That's where I leave you."

Andrew pursued his language fluency with the same drive he'd maintained over the past six years. After one wonderful meeting he testified that he'd spoken in Japanese "with the greatest freedom yet." He'd planned to speak on one topic but had suddenly chosen a different subject. No problem! He was now reaping the daily rewards of language proficiency. Finally, the Japanese words flowed through his mind like a deep and powerful stream. Best of all, he could now dip into it any time and in any way he wished.

By now he'd learned to build relaxing family time into his system. His early description of a vacation in Nikko shortly after he and Vera arrived in Japan proved that, with discipline, he knew how to accomplish a holiday. He praised the giant 1000-year-old maple trees on the hillsides in radiant autumn color. Foaming mountain streams and waterfalls. The long, easy mountain roads. The gorgeous golden temple. Even back in bustling Tokyo he could take time to visit the chrysanthemum show. He marveled at the unusual shapes of the mums, each plant featuring "boats," "autos," "cannon," and so forth. Thus, his keen sense of Nature's wonders had become even more refined. Back   there in Shintoistic Japan such appreciations were so basic to the culture

As he practiced the lighter side of holiday time, Andrew found a way to mix the profound and the silly. In later years in Japan, Lake Nojiri became the favorite holiday resort. Andrew and (later) his son Richard owned adjoining homes there. They were part of a seven-house community owned by the Seventh-day Adventist missionaries.

One day Andrew stood on the dock waiting for his family to come home from their excursion to the little island in the middle of the lake. Not unusually, he'd spent the morning with his books. Richard misjudged his arrival and sideswiped the boat landing. Several boards loosened and in an instant Andrew disappeared, almost. Standing up to his neck in the water and looking very surprised, he laughingly assured them that no real harm had been done. He could enjoy a joke as much as anyone else.

My Model
God is my systematic example.
He rules a systematic universe from his capital at its center.

Andrew N. Nelson

[1] P. A. Webber, "Japan Mission Training School," *Review & Herald* (April 9, 1920), p. 18.

7. The Great Tokyo Earthquake

Saturday, November 1, 1923, found the Nelson family in Takayama, their favorite beach resort at the time. They loved the way the rocky pine-clad hill ran almost all of the way down to the seashore. The worst storm of the summer had blown in that day, but that was nothing new. "The world, in general," Andrew wrote, "was running along on its usual schedule."

The previous night, however, he'd received a telegram from headquarters. "Come in to Tokyo. Committee." Had it not been Sabbath he would have set out immediately–business was always business with him. He would wait, however, and catch the night train to the city.

By sunset that evening, he was thankful to see that the rainstorm had let up. In the gloomy, black twilight Andrew set off on the six-mile hike to the nearest railway station. He picked his way along the road, boots squelching with every step in the gluey mud.

Briefly, a man with a lantern joined him, and they stumbled forward together. When it became clear that his companion had never before talked with a missionary, Andrew promptly did what he always did—introduced the man to Christianity. Then, at a fork in the road, they parted.

When the sky cleared a little more, Andrew was able to avoid the deepest mud holes, but the last stretch of the road was the worst. At the edge of town he stumbled into a teahouse to drink and take a little rest. Then, having scraped at least some of the mud off himself, he trudged on to the railway station.

The stationmaster stared at him. "I cannot sell you a ticket to Tokyo," he said.

"Well why not?" By now it was 8 o'clock at night, and Andrew had to find a way to Tokyo before committee time the next morning.

"Don't you know!" The man behind the brass grid shook his head. "There's been a great earthquake, and afterwards the whole city was destroyed by fire."

"What? When?" Secluded back among the rocks back at Ta-kayama the Nelsons had felt nothing.

The agent glanced up at the clock. "About eight hours ago."

Too late now to face the muddy journey back to his family that night, so Andrew bought a ticket to Sendai, just fifteen miles away. He knew that the Adventist home there would welcome him warmly. After he'd eaten some rice with them, they invited him to slip in under the same mosquito net with the whole family. Before they slept, how-ever, they prayed for all the friends and family members who, at that moment, were enduring who knew what troubles.

At 5:30 in the morning Andrew boarded the train back to the village where he'd started. Then he picked his way back over the same six muddy miles to rejoin his family at Takayama. He put up a notice on the bulletin board for the information of all of the other unknowing people in the resort.

Unable to believe the figure of 30,000 deaths, he announced that "about 15,000 people" had been killed." Forthwith his neighbors laughed him to scorn. "What do you mean, 15,000 people are dead!" To be sure, earthquakes were a familiar part of life in Japan, about four tremblers a day, actually. But surely it couldn't be *that* bad!

Whatever the number, Nelsons' summer vacation ended right there. Andrew packed up the family and took them home to Wakamatsu where they were stationed. It was a city in the mountains about eighty miles northwest of Takayama. The journey took three days. Along the way they saw refugees on the road—injured, hungry, thirsty. Some in rags. As they talked to eyewitnesses, they began to comprehend the magnitude of the tragedy. (In the end, the number of dead would be over 140,000, including the 40,000 who remained missing.) Many foreigners had been killed, about 5,000 of them. Yokohama was gone, and Tokyo had turned into a "living hell."

The next day, Wednesday, November 4, Andrew set out for Tokyo on the train. Never mind the committee. He *had* to know how everyone on the Amanuma compound had fared. He took his bicycle with him, although the ticketing cost almost as much as if he'd taken a person with him.

At Omiya, about an hour from Tokyo, everyone was ordered off the train. At first, Andrew thought he'd lost his bicycle. A quick prayer! The bike showed up in the middle of the confusion, before it would have disappeared for good. He tied his travel bag onto the back of it and faced the throng fleeing the city—bicycles, autos, pedestrians, carts. On to infinity. Everyone entering Tokyo had to bring with them enough food for three days. All of this misery was compounded by about 300 aftershocks each day—most of them, as Nelson put it, "unpleasantly hard."

On the Amanuma compound nearly everyone had been in church when the 8.3 earthquake struck at two minutes before noon. Accounts varied as to how long the quake lasted—anywhere from four to ten minutes.

For the moment, Victor Armstrong suggested to the congregation that the best they could do was stay in the church and pray. And so they did. Compared to most of the rest of the city, damage was surprisingly minimal. The church steeple bent itself over but otherwise held together. Also, for some days, families on compound would sleep in tents outside of their houses.

Nelson began to hear stories that turned out to be a succession of providences. Mrs. Kraft had missed church services that morning because she was sick. After the first jolt, however, she leaped out of bed and ran outside. Just after she passed the fireplace, the brick chimney collapsed behind her. Lila Armstrong, church pianist, had to cope with Beth. She took the baby home to nurse her, but the infant howled inconsolably. Therefore, taking her back into the church she handed Beth over to another lady in the congregation. When the Armstrongs returned home, they found that their chimney had collapsed and filled the empty baby buggy with bricks.

Since the disaster occurred at midday, many kitchen cookers were turned on. As the inevitable fires broke out, winds from a typhoon up north blew them into an inferno. With the water system destroyed, the firefighters' effectiveness was sorely limited. In one factory alone 4,000 people were incinerated. Two thirds of Tokyo lay in ruins with more than 300,000 houses burned. A tsunami near Yokohama killed 150. Several islands literally disappeared, and landslides swept away hillside homes. The financial loss was reckoned at five-and-a-half billion yen (one billion US dollars today).

In the wake of this enormous disaster the American Red Cross stepped in. "The U.S.A. is the most sympathetic nation in the world," one Tokyo newspaper declared. Japan's gratitude instantly improved U. S. Japanese relations.

The day after he reached Tokyo, Andrew set out for Yokohama on his bicycle to find the mother of one of his workers in Wakamatsu. Shortly, he and his colleague, Mr. Ed Kraft were stopped by soldiers who questioned them gruffly. Amid the chaos, rising panic all round threatened minority groups (especially the Koreans). For the moment everyone seemed to have assumed the authority to act like policemen.

When Nelson and Kraft finally arrived in the suburb of Higashi Kanagawa, they found the old lady safe in her house. The fires had suddenly stopped just one block short of her home. She and her servant had escaped furniture catapulting within the house. The two women managed to serve their guests rice and bean sauce—with *boiled* water. Almost as if life were normal—which it assuredly was *not*.

The men went on to examine the fate of the Japanese Signs of the Times Press. On any day other than Sabbath, employees would have been at work in the now-collapsed building. As it was, all had survived.

The entire city of Yokohama, however, was indeed gone. A vast spread of smoking ruins that might have been a forecast of Hiroshima's nuclear destruction twenty-two years into the future. To take pictures Nelson picked his way along the railway tracks where the earth had fallen away, leaving him fifteen feet above the ground. A dead horse here and bloated corpses there. The remains of streetcars lay inert by "naked" bridges. Looters were robbing the dead. Twenty-five charred bodies lay in the entrance of the Yokohama Bank building. (Seven hundred more who had taken refuge there had died inside.) "It is just too much to grasp!" Andrew afterwards groped for words to describe what he'd seen.

He spent another couple of days "straightening up" the school on the Amanuma compound. He had to rig up two sets of blocks and tackle and brought in many jacks to reset the house. With a crew of men at each rope and men at the jacks "that old building just came [back] into shape like a good boy," Andrew remembered

Meanwhile, he could get no news from his family up north. On one occasion, he was able to find powdered milk to send home for the twins. Also a yeast cake, because "Vera's starter had petered out." Still, no response came through.

Finally, Nelson began his journey home to Wakamatsu on November 21. He had to ride sixty-five miles on a torturous road before he could find a train on which he could carry his bike. Abandoning his faithful old bicycle was unthinkable. As he went, the vastness of the devastation hit Andrew all over again.

One after another, the stationmasters eyed his bicycle with

hostility. "No. You can't get on the train with that bicycle."

For hours he rode along dikes in the dark and crossed rivers, always moving in the general direction of home. So he plugged on "pedal-plug, plug-pedal, pedal-plug." His weary legs kept sending up messages to his brain that they'd "had enough." The hotels were full, and he couldn't even find a crate in which to ship his bicycle. About midnight, he secured a 3' by 6' "mat space" in a small inn.

The next day he reached Oyama and found that he could get on a train *with* his bike. Worn out but gratefully surprised, he found himself speeding away in a comfortable second-class coach.

The whole journey normally should have taken no more than ten hours. After that history-making Tokyo earthquake, he spent thirty-one hours on the way.

Home at last in Wakamatsu, he parked his bicycle in the shed and then crashed on what he later identified as a "real bed."

8. Japan Missionary College

When Andrew and Vera Nelson first arrived in Tokyo, the original Japanese training school had been closed for two years. A shortage of teachers was part of the problem.[1] It re-opened on October 1, 1919, however, under the management of Andrew and Perry Webber. They hoped to enroll thirty students but were much pleased to accept more than forty.   Still in language school himself, Nelson taught three English classes weekly. (That is nine classroom hours.)[2]

After several years of conducting what was essentially a boys' training school (Grades 7 – 12) on the crowded Tokyo compound, the mission committee decided to establish a more permanent college, away from the city. The Japan Mission purchased thirty-five acres of land (later expanded to forty-two acres) at Naraha, Chiba Ken, situated across the Bay some sixty miles southeast of Tokyo. The move promised to fulfill the "ideal of linking inseparably the physical, mental, and spiritual."[3]

Andrew Nelson was in the forefront of the plans, for these matters remained close to his heart for his entire life. Unwittingly, his personal background had prepared him well for the job of establishing a new college. He'd grown up working hard, accustomed to carrying much responsibility. From his carpenter father he'd learned basic house building and the rudiments of surveying. This knowledge became immediately useful when he had to prepare the hillside approach to the new campus and build a road into it.

Andrew actually spent a whole "bachelor year" working on this big project. When the Nelson family returned from their first furlough in August, 1926, they moved to the new school property.

While Andrew was not the first to advocate a school built according to the "blueprint," surely no one else had been more zealous for Christian education. Since his college years Andrew had been a diligent student of the Bible and the writings of Ellen White. From the book *Education* he gleaned several basic concepts. Plans must be made on a *large* scale. They must include more than simply "the pursuit of a certain course of study." Since true education involves eternity, it must prepare the student for service, both here and in the hereafter. The process must include the "harmonious development" of all human powers.

Fundamentals of Christian Education elaborated the specifics. Plan large. Create agricultural and manufacturing establishments. Build in the country, away from the turmoil of cities. Be near enough to the cities, however, to "do them good." All students, rich and poor, must engage in the work program. All teachers must spend some time working with the students. A spiritually strong program will build character and foster a spirit of evangelism. The total program must be scholastically superior and vocationally efficient.

Andrew was not, however, content to let the matter rest there and simply to pray for "a suitable place" to locate the new school. No! He set some very detailed specifications before the Almighty.

A Prayer List for *Nihon Saniku Gakuin*
(Japan Missionary College)

1. A quiet place in the country
2. A good road leading into the property
3. Space for a four square-mile campus
4. A beautiful, inspiring view
5. Level building sites
6. Fertile land to raise a variety of crops
7. Plenty of water and year-round rain
8. A large forest for lumbering
9. Electricity (this, Lord, is a necessity these days)
10. No malaria
11. No typhoons
12. No dangerous, anti-government groups nearby

In the interest of saving money and fostering the work-study program, the small faculty decided to build their own homes, as well as all of the school buildings. In those "eager early days," of course, a few things went wrong. In their haste, they built the woodworking shop in a single day. The next day it fell down! The arrival of the permanent carpentry teacher, Myron Powers, prevented further mishaps of that kind.

For the first chapel service Nelson depicted Christ as the Carpenter of Nazareth. Exhilarated, the small group of pioneering young men responded with enthusiasm. Soon homes and buildings began popping up all over the lovely campus. Rich crops on the student-cultivated farm provided food for all. Students also trained as firefighters, with equipment provided by the grateful community. They became adept at putting out nearby forest fires.

The school days began with a general meeting in the conference room at 7:35. After prayers and announcements, the work program for the day was lined up. Then came the great scattering of people to the workshops, woods, gardens, and classrooms.

Reviewing the first eleven years of Japan Junior College gave Andrew Nelson justifiable satisfaction. Teachers, accountants, secretaries, and translators had graduated. Industrial offerings included carpentry, metalwork, farming, dairy, printing, canning, cooking, and so forth. The Church and all of its departments had benefited from many evangelistic enterprises. The Girls School sponsored a most interesting vocational occupation, the commercial production of *kimonos*. Nothing could be more beautiful or more ethnically Japanese.

All of the school buildings, shops and dwellings had been "homemade." Perhaps the most exciting event, however, occurred in 1927 when an official letter arrived from Pastor Victor Armstrong, Chairman of the Board. Addressed to the "Faculty and Student Body of Japan Missionary College," it asked the teachers and students to come to town and to build the new Tokyo Sanitarium and Hospital. (They did it!)

Pressure to establish a strong faculty occupied much of Nelson's time. Sometimes the needs of the college could be quite overwhelming. In the first place, Japan's "lack of progress" was caused by "an absence of trained young workers." Students enrolling in a Christian college, were often disowned by their Buddhist families. This meant that provision had to be made for them to become self-supporting.

Vera's lovely domestic touch could be felt in so many ways on campus. Among other things, she taught conversational English classes to many of the Japanese young people who needed help. Then she would sponsor Saturday evening parties where she served home-made fudge, popcorn, apples and other traditional buffet foods. The Number One Party Rule was that no one should speak anything but English while in the house.

On one occasion a young man saw a single rose, gleaned from Vera's ever-flourishing flower garden. He went over to the piano where it stood in a little vase. Without saying a word, he returned to his seat. After spending some time with his dictionary, he put together an English sentence—in fact, a rapturous one. With great gallantry he stood up and declared: "What a beautiful stink!"

On consideration, perhaps that was one of the most sincere tributes Vera's beloved garden ever received.

At this time, high school education was already common in Japan. Therefore, many students arrived ready to work at college level. This situation demanded a strong faculty. Moreover, as many girls as boys were seeking entrance, and the student population soon stood at 100. Finding good teachers was essential because weak staffing would mean a loss of confidence in the school. Maintaining a good reputation had to be high priority.

In due course, two more American families arrived. Francis Millard took care of both agriculture and financing as well as evangelistic work. Talented in both piano and choir, his wife Fern started a music department. Clarence Thurston taught business, and his wife Rachel gave instruction in the arts.

Understandably, all of this activity and determination had caused Andrew to step on a few toes along the way. "If we had any more men like Nelson," one pessimist grumbled, "we'd wreck the whole denomination."

Having already affirmed his own "Master Plan," Andrew took the criticism in stride. "So! After eleven years of service in Japan, I have joined the ranks of the undesirables?" he remarked. "Though I don't feel that it is my fault, I can consider it as a compliment. Perhaps it is because I worked so hard to get a suitable faculty lined up for the college." He mused mildly, "Prayer will repair even this attitude, so I am not overly concerned. May God who has granted my requests [so far] make it successful. I am sure He will."

Throughout those pioneer years, an occasional Nelson family–crisis itself into the foreground with startling urgency. One night Vera, complaining of a pain in her right side, woke her husband. "It may be appendicitis," she told him in a rather matter-of-fact way.

Fully aware of his wife's canny insights, however, Andrew bounded out of bed and away. By 2:56 a.m., he carefully recorded, he was on his way to Kisarazu on his bicycle, his only means of the transportation. He peddled past shadowy trees and sleeping villages, a lantern swinging from the handlebars. More than once, when he crashed to the ground on the rough road, he had to pick himself up, search for a match and candle, and re-light the lantern. Presently, the red moon arose, casting sullen shadows across the rice fields.

Suddenly a bright light pierced the gloom. The police who ambushed him wanted to know what a foreigner was doing out on the road at this time of night. "I'm trying to get to Kisarazu to rent a car and get my wife to the hospital," Andrew cried in frustration. Indeed, the cops stopped him two more times before he reached his destination.

Having rented a new Chevrolet he hastily retraced the road back to Naraha. In the clear light of day, he finally reached home to find that Vera's appendix had already ruptured. With time scarcely to draw a breath, he settled her into the back seat of the car and rushed back to Kisarazu. Providentially, the doctor on duty in the Emergency Room that morning shift was able to operate and save her life.

Less traumatic but equally consuming of time and emotion was the everyday business of rearing the three children. Ever the true wife and household manager, Vera arose capably to every occasion. The children filled their days with new episodes.

At age six Richard entered Grade 1 in Mrs. Powers' little elementary school. Soon, she sent him home. "He's just not ready for school." The same thing happened when he was seven. Now his parents began to worry about this "slow learning" child.

Even if he couldn't yet read, Richard already exhibited an uncanny mechanical sense. One day Andrew came home to find that Richard had done a great job of organizing his tools. "How did you manage to sharpen the cross-cut saw," he inquired.

"Easy," Richard replied. "Since every other tooth is different, I just skipped over every other one. So, after sharpening one side that way, I turned the saw over and sharpened every other one on that side." Andrew stared down at his little son, amazed. "Don't worry, Papa. I held the file correctly."

Finally, at the summer resort when he was eight years old,

Richard noticed that all of the other children his age could read. They could just look at the bulletin board and know what was going on! Promptly he decided that he might be missing something. When he started school in the fall, he went through three grades in one year.

Actually, the first son of the Nelson family could be quite an operator. He'd get up for "work" about dawn. Why so *early*, his parents wondered. "You see," he replied, when I wake up in the morning, I stay awake in bed for awhile, thinking about what we're going to do today." He monitored his activities according to the time when the rising sun hit a certain square in his window. "When it's right there," he explained, "I get up and go out to get the things we have ready."

His self-appointed "duties" included enterprises like trying to catch the school dog and hitch him to the wagon. (Not a success.) His lucky days were the cloudy ones when the sun couldn't shine in the window pane. Then he didn't have to get up to work.

When the twins were five, Vera nursed them through chicken pox. Surprisingly, they decided to stop squabbling and became "a loving couple." Dorothy smothered Donald with hugs and kisses, murmuring "O, you sweet little Donald!" Because he was at the time smaller, she always gave him the biggest of everything. He always took the biggest too, chirping, "Dorty loves me, and I love Dorty."

Having no one but boys to play with, Dorothy could more than hold her own. She paid attention to her dolls only when her brothers would play with her. She could run, climb, dig in the dirt, and turn somersaults with the best of them. In yet another burst of maturity Dorothy could dress and undress herself long before the fearful Donald would even try.

In 1929 a very wonderful event occurred. Andrew Nelson's former roommate at Walla Walla College, Joe Hall, sent the family a much-needed gift. A new car! The Model A Ford was certainly a great family joy and a personal relief. (It recalled that terrible night when Vera almost died of a ruptured appendix, all for the lack of a car.)

Moving up from the bicycle (and train) to a private car had, indeed, been a truly heady experience. Even so, Andrew's resourcefulness could still be taxed. One very dark summer night, he and one of the Japanese pastors were heading home. Suddenly, a tire blew. The men got out of the car, Andrew chiding himself for getting caught without even a flashlight. Not a star or even the sliver of a moon.

Resignedly, he squatted down by the wheel. "How am I supposed to do this in the dark? No reply. He realized that his friend had wandered off somewhere. "At least, he could have stayed by me. Guess I have to do this alone and by Braille." Blind and clumsy, he started to loosen the lug nuts, hoping not to lose any of them in the rutted, roadside mud.

Suddenly, a soft glow of white light enveloped him and the Model A. He looked up to see the pastor carefully holding the four corners of his handkerchief. It was full of fireflies! Andrew reminded himself, again, not to pre-judge anyone's intentions.

So, in that ethereal light Andrew finished his mundane job of changing the tire. Then his innovative friend shook out his handkerchief, releasing a brilliant shower of fireflies. Now, everyone could go home!

A couple of years later the beloved car involved the Nelsons in yet one more miracle. One that burned itself into their minds for life. The whole family had driven the long road around Tokyo Bay for a day of shopping, meeting medical appointments and transacting business for the college. Late at night, on the way home, they approached a familiar railway crossing. The guard had already gone to bed, so Andrew stopped, rolled down the windows, and stared into the rain, and listened. Nothing.

He pulled ahead. Then the train burst out of the fog, on top of them, its kerosene headlamp feebly winking in the murky air. It missed by about five feet.

Shaken to the core, Andrew pulled to the side of the road and stopped. "We must thank God, children." The words caught in his throat. "He still has something for all of us to do." Everyone would relive that moment and vividly remember Andrew's prayer.

The Model A proved to be a huge campus asset. After all, the Naraha Railway Station was two miles away. The everlasting bicycles that swarmed over the countryside might accomplish much, but certainly not everything.

Early on, Andrew Nelson realized that all of the hard work and the rushing from one task to another had taken "much of the cream out of life." Constantly he fought his tendency to overbook his time and his energies. Daily forced himself to "plan less in a given amount of time. "When a thing is determined upon," he sighed, "I am always driven to leave the old and appropriate the new."

As already recorded, he literally had to train himself to take family vacations. The day he drove the new Model A Ford to their Takayama, their favorite holiday destination, was indeed a very, very happy venture. That's where they once saw a brilliant blue–green meteor fall. Even more importantly, they watched Halley's Comet which comes by only once in seventy-five years. Light shows in the heavens never failed to thrill Andrew. At the same time, he learned to thoroughly enjoy the very human pleasure of having a corn roast on the beach along with his fellow missionaries. On a daily basis at home he loved to retreat into the company of his library books.

[1] Irwin H. Evins, "A Month in Japan," *Review & Herald* (September 4, 1919), pp. 15-16. Perry A. Webber took over the leadership of the school.
[2] P. A. Webber, "Japan Mission Training School," *Review & Herald* (April 29, 1920), p. 18.
[3] *Far Eastern Division Outlook* (October, 1926), pp. 2-3.

9. Furlough, Academics, and Flood

The Nelsons' first home-leave was due in the fall of 1925. The Church's policy on home leaves appears to have adopted a kind of Biblical connotation: Seven years of labor was to be followed by the "Jubilee Year" (Lev. 25:2-4). The Nelsons, then, were due a one-year furlough after seven years of service in Japan.

Despite all of Vera's vigilance and domestic skills, however, the twins, Donald and Dorothy, had developed rickets. Lively little tots they were, but their bowed legs boded no good. Ever since the great earthquake finding a balanced and sufficient diet was a constant challenge. The children were simply not thriving. It was decided, therefore, that Vera leave early and take the children back to home base in Seattle.

Meanwhile, Andrew would keep on doing what he was doing (for almost a year), establishing the new Japanese college in Chiba Ken. On June 21, 1924, he stood on the dock in Yokohama and watched the ship carry away his entire family.[1] Technically, the Nelsons' first furlough had begun, but it certainly didn't feel anything like a jubilee.

Back home and surrounded by all of the grandparents and other loving relatives, Vera was able to augment the family income a little. It would help with purchases they would need to make before returning to Japan. She found a job nursing at the local hospital in Kent, Washington, and also in Seattle

Many months later Andrew arrived to reunite the family.

Well–ordered as his private, family, and professional life might be, however, young Professor Nelson still had a few fine points to master. His little sister Vivian always remembered the morning her adored big brother "took a lickin'" from their Mama Gustava, so to speak.

During this, their first furlough from Japan, the family lived in the basement apartment at 1208 Shelby Street. One Saturday morning, the constant blaring of a car horn split the air in the usually peaceful lakeside community. Dressed and ready to go, Andrew sat at the wheel. He fully intended to get to church on time.

Immediately, the front door burst open and Mama Nelson darted down the steps, her face getting more red with every stride down to the curb. "Asch! So what for are you sitting there making noise?" she demanded.

Suddenly feeling a very small boy again, Andrew murmured, "But, Mama, we're going to be late."

"No but me!" Gustava gripped the car door in high heat. "You get back down there with Vera and all of those babies. You want to be on time? You go *help* her get ready."

Having no answer to the charges, Andrew obediently returned to the house. He could hear his mother, following close behind. "You *help* her, see? Three of them . . ." No one, including Andrew himself, had seen her more upset.

By the time he reached home for his furlough year, Andrew had formulated an ambitious plan for himself. Driven by his zeal for learning he embarked on doctoral studies at the University of Washington. At this time, earning a PhD was a rarity–something that only a few very serious, intellectual persons undertook. Most people considered a high-school diploma to be a perfectly satisfactory end point to their education.

Beyond that, a dark suspicion of higher education lurked in many places within the Seventh-day Adventist church. If you couldn't secure your training within a church institution, then you'd better not go out at all. Whether or not Andrew Nelson ever paid any attention to this prejudice we cannot tell. Probably he didn't. All we know is that by 1926 he'd already distinguished himself as a linguist, teaching Japanese as a foreign language at the University of Washington (in the Department of Oriental History).

With typical foresight he had formulated a major plan for his future research. His years in Japan had already thoroughly saturated his observant nature with not only the language but also the culture. Ever sensitive to religious impulses, he would ultimately entitle his dissertation "The Origin, History, and Present Status of the Temples of Japan." (He received his Ph.D. in 1938.)

Nelson understood the simple teachings of Shinto that advocated "Deeds rather than creeds." Although mixed with Buddhism and Confucianism, that native religion expressed itself, for example, in the prevalence of natural, unpainted wood. It captured the very "essence of trees" and dictated that a tall, tiered pagoda, like a tree, had a central pillar within itself. Shintoism affirmed just four uncomplicated principles: (1) Observation of annual festivals, (2) Reverence for tradition and family, (3) The worship of *kami* (sacred spirits of Nature) at shrines, and (4) Physical cleanliness.

Nelson's years of in-depth research would involve architectural studies and hours of interviews. It would uncover information unavailable even in Japanese print, let alone English.

Before the end of their furlough year, Andrew performed the wedding ceremony for his brother Reuben and Fay Stokes (August 25, 1925). It was the first of several weddings out of 1208 that he, the preacher in the family, celebrated. At the same time, he found his sister Gertrude and her husband George Bergman preparing to go as missionaries to Ethiopia.

It took persistence and courage to return to Japan in 1926.[2] Nonetheless, Andrew Nelson resumed his job as principal of Japan Junior College with a will.[3] Sometimes, though, the weight of all of the other duties almost overwhelmed him. One time he expressed great gratitude when all he had to do–in addition to the principalship– was to be business manager, teach four classes, lead out in Harvest Ingathering and supervise field–work.

Andrew recognized Providence whenever and however it visited him. One day he lost his wallet on his way to Yokohama. "God sent it back to me via two dogs and a patient in the Sanitarium." The first dog brought it back in a downpour of rain and deposited it on the Sanitarium lawn. Another dog came up and fought for it, scattering the contents far and wide—40 yen ($12), his driver's license and so forth. From his bed a patient watched the fracas and came down to pick up the debris. The dogs ran off with the tattered but now-empty wallet. "Wonderful!" Andrew exclaimed. "How thankful I am!"

Whatever the public demands, Andrew always knew exactly what was going on at home. For the family's convenience he invented a "furnace starter" for cold winter mornings. After setting a fire in the floor furnace, he attached a weighted string to the moving part of an old-fashioned alarm clock and fastened the other end to the damper.

When the alarm rang, the weight dropped, and the clapper hit the bell. The movement was enough to lift the damper and light the fire. Everyone could then wake up to a warm house.

As for the children, they worked according to the weekly "Work Chart." (see Appendix I, p. 136.) In Andrew Nelson's carefully managed household there was no space left for idleness, bad manners, or "attitude." The three children's daily opportunity to practice these virtues began at 6:30 each morning.

They were so disciplined that they could be left alone when their parents had to go into Tokyo. During their absence Donald and Dorothy would figure out what surprise they could make for their parents. Sometimes they'd organize the attic, sometimes the basement. They'd sit waiting at the window, through supper and beyond. If they were in bed before the Model A Ford chugged back into the garage, they'd have to jump up to show off their accomplishments. Their father's enthusiastic response was always the reward. "Wonderful!" he'd exclaim. "The Gold Dust Twins have been at work again!" The children lived for their Dad's commendations.

Andrew never failed to tell people that he appreciated them. When the Thurstons and Millards gave him a "lovely surprise party" for his thirty-seventh birthday, he rejoiced in the "fine spirit" they always brought with them. "It did me a world of good!" he recalled. As usual, a heavy workday lay ahead of them all, so eating the strawberries and cake for breakfast seemed perfectly logical timing.

In that same birthday month, however, Andrew had to suffer the kind of loss that many missionaries in faraway places have endured. His mother Gustava died. She "slipped peacefully away," he wrote, "surrounded by friends and loved ones in the Portland Sanitarium." She was 4,000 miles away, and he was not among them. The family, however, had all "showered" her with cheery letters for her recent November 24, 1931, birthday. That evening he stepped out into his garden in Japan under his "sympathetic pine trees." The "bright green needles" shone in the January sun and made him remember his mother's purity and love. Somehow it flowed like "a silver stream of joy" that took away the sting, until he was able to check the tears and "be able to be up and at my work."

In 1932 workers in Japan next had to endure yet another natural disaster. Wedged in between the coast and a beautiful range of hills, the port city of Kobe was no stranger to earthquakes, of course.

Perhaps the Hanshin Earthquake (6,400 dead) that year triggered the insane rainfall that lasted for weeks in mid-summer. On Tuesday, July 5, someone estimated that three gallons of water fell upon each square foot of the city. "Anyone wearing spectacles would have to be fitted with windshield wipers," Fellow-missionary Dietrich observed wryly, "if he wanted to see anything at all."

As he had done after the Tokyo Earthquake nine years earlier, Andrew Nelson hastened to the stricken city to look out for the welfare of his beloved church people. He had to choose between reaching Kobe by a boat or trying a combination of bus, tram, and walking. When he arrived in Osaka, he found the government trains creeping along the quadruple railway line in single file. They switched from one track to another to avoid washouts and fallen rocks. The twenty-one mile journey took two-and-a-half hours.

He couldn't believe what he saw. How could a city set on a hill with scarcely a level site within it perish in a flood? Many days of continuous rain were topped off with a relentless, seven-hour downpour. The earth revolted. When men left for work at eight o'clock that morning Kobe's swift streams looked, perhaps, a little larger, but the conduits were still safely draining off the surplus. Just one hour later people were isolated everywhere on "islands" of misery. Tremendous landslides brought down tons of earth, boulders and trees. Two of the city's three dams broke and twenty new rivers roared down through the city, some a quarter of a mile wide. Before this enormous tide of destruction stood at least 180,000 of Kobe's beautiful homes.

Dr. Elmer Olson had also left his home at 8 a.m. for his office in the little Nunobiki Sanitarium. He stood helpless as the stream he'd just crossed turned into a torrent. Houses crumbled before his eyes and what had been a tidy community turned into a seething mass of furniture, rugs, trinkets, timbers, and trash. He saw the under-pinning of his own home fall away. Frantically, he motioned for his wife, standing at the front, to flee for her life.

Mistakenly, she thought he wanted her to take their valuables upstairs. In the middle of that operation the kindly man next door also tried to persuade her to leave. Still unaware of the imminent danger, she kept dragging things upstairs. The neighbor decided to help her, and they even hauled the large Chinese rug up to the next floor. Again he urged her to leave. Thinking she was doing her best, Winona Olson insisted on packing a suitcase to carry food and clothes for the baby.

Finally, the distraught doctor watched his wife with the baby and the neighbor with the suitcase climb out of an upstairs window. They first jumped onto the roof of the shed and from there to higher ground. Almost immediately thereafter the whole house tumbled into the new river and crashed down into what had formerly been a quarry pit. There it buried itself deep in the mud.

The couple's eventual safe reunion made all of their losses seem very small. Oddly enough, the Chinese rug was recovered. After cleaning it was good as new. Nothing else material, however, remained of the Olsons' pre-flood lives.

Through it all, none of the Adventist church members were among the hundreds of people who died that day. Also, the mission headquarters remained in tact. From there, relief work began at once. The women's societies in all of the churches gathered clothes and household utensils for those who had lost all. Dr. Olson offered to give free examinations and vaccinations and to provide every possible medical service within his reach.

Once more the Mission personnel suffered material loss. Still, Providence preserved their lives—and that was enough.

[1] *Far Eastern Division Outlook* (August, 1924), p. 12.
[2] In 1926 Seventh-day Adventist church membership for the whole of Japan still stood at just 482, with only ten organized churches.
[3] *Far Eastern Division Outlook* (October, 1926), p. 2.

10. Travel as Living History

When the Nelson family's second furlough came due in August 1933, the children were old enough to take a keen interest in everything that happened. In her diary, ten-year-old Dorothy recalled one last-minute event before they left Japan. They stopped at a mosque where her father took half an hour to talk one more time to one of his Moslem friends "about Jesus." So typical of Andrew Nelson's mindset. After that, they took the train for Yokohama where they boarded the Japanese freighter *Katsu Maru*.

At a leisurely pace unknown to contemporary air-travelers, the Nelsons settled their luggage in their two cabins, roamed around the ship for a few hours and went up on deck for the 5:00 p.m. sailing. Out beyond the breakwater they cruised down Tokyo Bay, the familiar lighthouses along the shore winking at them.

As civilian passengers they ate their meals in the Officers' Dining Room. In the traditions of sea travel, the officers were usually very friendly with the children aboard. The Chief Engineer took them down to the engine room. Although much of the information was lost on the children, certainly Andrew himself would not have missed any of the fine points. Another day they were invited up onto the bridge where Andrew and Vera even had the chance to telegraph their relatives. It particularly pleased their father that up there his children were shown the ship's exact position by pointing the sextant to the stars.

In the open sea, watching schools of porpoises far outstripped the interest of any other passing ships. On good days the kids jumped rope on the deck. When the weather was rough and the foghorn blew non-stop, the children stayed inside. They played a lot of ping-pong, as well as the table games their parents had wisely brought with them. The voyage did, however, prove to be somewhat over-long. The company had decided to save money by *not* having the barnacles scraped off the last time the worthy *Katsu Maru* had been berthed in New York.

Eventually, they crossed the Dateline, on Sabbath. Which day to keep? Actually, the Nelsons decided that keeping *two* Sabbaths in succession seemed a very good way to spend the time.

Before the ship first made land in San Pedro, everyone could smell the late summer forest fires burning in California. Relatives in Los Angeles took them home overnight. There Vera became the object of laughter when, on the street, she tapped on the window of a parked car window calling to the driver, "*Anoneh, anoneh*! ("Your attention, sir"). The man, understandably, was mystified. Andrew and Vera discovered that after fourteen years in Japan they might expect some culture shock when they came home.

Once more at sea, the ship followed the Mexican coast down toward the entrance of the Panama Canal. Dorothy never forgot her Daddy pointing out the beauties of shore as they sailed south. The spouting whales, of course—but much more. "The wake of the moon," he wrote, "finally evaporated in the glistening sea . . . and presented us with the most remarkable reflecting spectacle I've ever seen. It was fireworks on the water! Yellow and bluish sparks showered over the surface of the nearby waves and boat swells."

On the way, a crisis occurred in the engine room. One of the engineers, Date San, severely burned his hand when hot oil shot out of a broken pipe. With her usual concern, Vera tried to relieve his pain. When gangrene set in, the Nelsons twice tried to persuade the Captain to stop so that the crewman could be put ashore and receive treatment. The answer was always shockingly and depressingly the same: "It is impossible."

At last, at the Pacific end of the Panama Canal, Date San was deposited at a large government hospital for the surgery that he by then desperately needed.

At 6 a.m. on September 13 they passed through two rows of buoys and into the Canal. The whole family went up onto the bridge to watch the air show–three little planes chasing one another overhead. The real excitement, however, was passing through the locks. Watching the gates opening and shutting and the water alternately bubbling up and draining away became a full time occupation until they reached the Atlantic side.

In due course, the Caribbean islands, Florida, and the Bahamas gave way to the Gulf Stream, followed by a few days of landless travel. Finally, the Statue of Liberty welcomed them into New York.

There Andrew Nelson picked up a brand new 1933 Chevy for the rest of their journey. As a furloughing missionary, he fulfilled numerous church and camp meeting appointments. In Brooklyn he preached in English for the first time in seven years.

When they visited the Review and Herald Publishing House in Takoma Park, they slept at the Washington Sanitarium and much enjoyed the excellent cafeteria food there. In fact, the food in the many homes where they were guests tasted utterly exotic.

They detoured up to New England to see the marvelous autumn colors and visit the many historic sites. They also acquired a jar of the world's best maple syrup. All in all, these travels became a living lesson book in American history and culture, all new to the three Japanese-nurtured Nelson children.

Adventist history came into focus in Michigan. Then, not surprisingly, Andrew wanted to visit every church college in the whole country. Of Southern Junior College he said: "This proves to be the best of the colleges we visited. It is the most balanced and up and coming school." Invariably he looked into all of the work-study programs. He admired the industries at Union College, Nebraska. He spoke twice at Southwestern Junior College in Keene, Texas, pronouncing it "a wide-awake school."

Wisely, the Nelson family had furnished themselves with a tent and mosquito net for the long, cross-country journey to Seattle. At $3.00 a night hotels were unthinkable. Finally, 100 miles west of Carlsbad Caves in New Mexico, the trunk fell off the back of the car. For the rest of the way, it had to ride on the front bumper, with thirteen-year-old Richard sitting up front and holding the trunk in place. This measure caused the radiator to overheat. Hence, getting out of the desert, finally, came as a great relief.

The Rockies and the redwood forests along with visits with friends in Southern California took up more days. On December 12 they stopped for a week with Andrew's sister Vivian at Pacific Union College. (As usual Andrew visited industries and classes.)

Heavy rains welcomed them to Washington State. They arrived at Vera's childhood home in Kent with rainwater "up over the wheels . . . [and] rolling like an inverted Niagara Falls over the hood of the car." On the very last day of 1933, the Nelson car stopped in front of the 1208 Shelby Street home in Seattle. Andrew blew the horn. There they saw Papa Andrew Nelson standing—alone—at the front door.

Since leaving Yokohama four months earlier they had traveled 20,000 miles!

After the New Year, the three children entered "a real school." Richard went into Grade 7, but where should the twins go? With tutoring (home-schooling) they'd completed five grades in four years. Since almost half the year was already gone, they both just slid into Grade 5 again. With all of the exciting sights and sounds of a big school engulfing them, kids didn't care one way or the other.

Happily, they all moved into the old family home. (Grandpa took an upstairs room for the time being.) Although the Great Depression was in full swing, Andrew Nelson had the security of a regular furlough salary—for his second seven-year term of service in Japan. Also, he earned a little extra income helping his father on carpentry jobs.

Reuniting with friends and family, of course, has always been one of the intended restorative virtues of the furlough year. Near the end of their time in Seattle they spent a few days on the campus of their Alma Mater, Walla Walla College (Andrew graduated in 1914 and Vera in 1916).[1] Bonding with one's classmates is, of course, a well–documented, lifelong benefit. At that time, the Far Eastern Division was well populated with alumni of Walla Walla College. In fact, just the previous year, Andrew and Vera had joined nine of their classmates in Japan in sending greetings to their College for campus homecoming in the spring of 1933.[2] As it turned out, the next Nelson to attend Walla Walla College would be young Richard, their elder son.

Meanwhile, Andrew kept the two main interests of his life constantly before him. On many weekends he preached in area churches. Visits to the nearby grave of his mother, Mama Nelson, always blended astronomy and the gospel in his thinking: "Far above, high in the sky, are the stars," he mused, "[but she's] . . . not floating around in the ether, according to the heathen ideas of America and the Orient. No, she is resting quietly from her work, and when mine is finished at the end of the world, I'll join her when Jesus wakes us up. [Then] we'll go home together." His disciplined mind always reverted to what he called "common sense and sure religion of the Bible."

Naturally, the ever-scholarly Andrew checked in with the university and was assured that his PhD program was on track. Gleefully, he reported the purchase of a new Underwood typewriter for $70. (It had been listed for $105.) "Now I can type my own dissertation . . . on the subject of 'The Religions of Japan.'"

As it turned out, it would be Richard the teenager who would type the final copy of that very complex document. Necessarily, the dissertation combined English and *Kanji* (Chinese characters).[3]

[1] *North Pacific Union Gleaner* (July 3, 1934), p. 8.
[2] *North Pacific Union Gleaner* (June 13, 1933), p. 8.
[3] *Kanji* are the Chinese characters used in the modern Japanese writing system. Other elements are *Hiragana, Katakana,* and Indo-Arabic numerals. Occasionally *Romaji* (Latin alphbet) is used. Additionally, a single *Kanji* character may have multiple readings. Thus, Japanese writing becomes very complex.

11. A Manifesto for a College of Power

Furlough time ended late in August, 1934. In some ways it had been like eating dessert every day, but now the whole Nelson family looked forward to being home again in Japan. With the suitcases unpacked. With familiar surroundings and predictable routines.

No one, at that time, could predict the rocky road that they would have to walk before the end of their third term of service. Dark clouds were rolling up over the horizon, but even a practiced Japan–watcher like Andrew Nelson had no way of fully understanding what they meant.

At the annual Far Eastern Division meetings held in Manila in 1935 the administrators voted Nelson to a two-year term as a member of the Division Committee. He confidently considered the appointment as "an interesting and profitable experience." Had he realized that he might be moving, even temporarily, away from the college scene that he so loved, he might have been a little anxious. By now the enrollment had increased to 500. Things went well at Japan Missionary College

Like an attentive parent, Andrew reviewed the work of the past decade. He described the practical application of his theories of Christian education. The "judicious combination of theory and practice" had been graduating young men and women who could survive "even in times like these." He proudly gave the beautiful Naraha campus the title of "The College of Power."

Few others have set forth their ideals in a more organized or detailed manner. Nelson didn't claim, in every respect, to have yet attained all of the heights. Still, he certainly envisioned a time, "ere long," when the school would be running smoothly along these lines.

A Manifesto for the College of Power

A. The School Estate

1. The campus is set back a quarter-mile on a wooded road. A neatly woven wire fence surrounds the entire property.
2. A triple-arched entrance spans the automobile road and two gravel paths. A painting set into each archway, is protected from the weather.
   a. *Center:* An open Bible (moral training)
   b. *Left*: A student studying in the spacious library (mental training)
   c. *Right*: A mechanical workshop (physical training)
3. A large tract of natural forest has been preserved, framing a view of a snow-capped Mt. Fuji.
4. Lawns, shrubbery and flower-beds define the campus boundaries.
5. Three substantial, attractive buildings stand on the circle driveway
   a. *Central*. Chapel and Church, include the pastor's offices, the Bible classrooms, and rooms for missionary activities.
   b. *Left*. Library and most of the classrooms. On the right, the offices of the president and his staff, the treasurer and his accountants.
   c. *Right*. Vocational building. Behind are grouped various commercial shops (printing, woodworking, health-food factory and various agricultural buildings.)
6. Two smaller buildings occupy the spaces between the three main structures:
   a. The Hall of Music (All students required to have some music training.)
   b. The Sanitarium
7. The School Farm gradually is expanding to include all 500 acres of the estate, with the exception of the border of forest and the campus itself.

B. The Educational Program

1. The school operates twelve months a year (four quarters)
2. Grades 11 to 14. The enriched program, however, may keep a student at work for four to six years.
3. A faculty of specialists, each with personal responsibility for mentoring students.
4. A flexible program gives a student a balanced education.
   a. Three days a week: Study, theory, and preparation
   b. Two days a week (alternating): Work, practice and experience.
5. Triple program each day.
   a. Morning: Mental and spiritual studies
   b. Afternoon: Vocational classes
   c. Library and laboratory work
6. Eight-hour workdays for mature students. Younger students work less and have some hours of supervised study.
7. Student labor is paid. Provision here for even the "unwealthy."
   a. Commercial shops run every weekday.
   b. Students desiring to build up financial credit faster may defer studies for a quarter and work full time.

C. Methodology

1. Laboratory method used. No conventional question-and-answer recitations or "parroting" of the teacher.[1]
2. Direct study and group discussions. Each student has a faculty mentor who advises according to financial and mental capabilities.
3. Early to bed and early to rise.
4. Occasional social events
5. Evenings for elective reading, not heavy study periods.
6. Graduates from the College of Power will have three majors:
    a. Mental/literary studies
    b. Moral/spiritual (Bible)
    c. Vocational/physical (minor trades and healthful living)

D. School Finance

1. Three Sources of Income:
    a. Industrial earnings,
    b. Income from students. (Board, room and tuition, but no extra fees.)
    c. Subsidy as needed. Aim that school operations will be self-supporting.
2. The work-study program enables all students to earn either part or all of their own way through school. They are to be paid according to the quality and quantity of their work.

On the eve of graduation day in 1936, Andrew Nelson sat under his pine trees at Naraha, with Mt Fuji looking down upon him. He felt deep satisfaction after his ten years of pioneering in education. His ideas of what a Seventh-day Adventist school should be like had been vindicated. Truly, he said, "our school has come to stay." Not only had the Korean Mission asked for help in establishing *their* new college, but his policies had attracted international attention. His ideals actually "worked." An invigorating and hopeful thought, to be sure.[2]

As the new (eleventh) school year opened, enrollment went up by 20%. Every-thing was running like a well-tuned engine. Still, all was not well. Andrew sat in his study, his 600 books all nearly arranged on the shelves, thinking.

His colleague, Victor Armstrong, had been chosen as the new president of the Far Eastern Division. Because of the on-going political uncertainties the Division offices were being moved from Shanghai to Singapore, an obviously secure place. That was all right. The hard part, however, was the fact that Andrew had been elected to replace him as president of the Japan Mission. A very disappointing development and one shared by the entire college family. "Might I not stay?" Andrew complained in his journal.[3]

Nonetheless, like the troopers they were, the Nelson family moved to Tokyo at the end of the school year. He then brought his friend Francis Millard out to the "old stamping ground" and turned the school administration over to him. In March the government had given Japan Missionary College official recognition. That news delighted everyone, in spite of the personal adjustments that were going on within the Japan Mission organization.

A few months later—in their new work–Andrew and Vera visited Singapore for the Division Committee.[4] While there they witnessed the particularly "terrible atonement ceremony" of Thaipusam at a Hindu temple. The devotees with spears in their backs, brass hooks on their chests, and long needles through their cheeks and tongues walked the streets. This ghastly effort "to obtain salvation" utterly appalled the Nelsons.

Meanwhile, a forecast of things to come began to appear in the affairs of Far Eastern Academy in Shanghai, China. This rather unusual secondary school had been provided by the Division for the children of missionaries. The students came home at Christmas and during summer vacations and were handsomely provided for on campus the rest of the year. To this day, hundreds of former students will testify that "FEA" was the best place in the whole world to go to school. All three of the young Nelsons loved the place—Richard in Grade 12 and the twins finishing Grade 8.

Andrew surveyed his children with a practiced eye. Editor of both the school paper and the annual, Richard was also president of the senior class. Indeed, his persistent hard work, leadership abilities, and accurate workmanship admirably reflected the skills of his father. "He's a conscientious Christian . . . He can type 70 or 80 words a minute with only one or two mistakes, in the duration of ten minutes. He can write 80 words a minute in shorthand with accuracy. He learned printing in the FEA print shop. He learned plumbing with me."

And the second son? He'd been president of his 8th-grade class. His father Andrew still considered that his "main responsibility is to make a good man out of Donald. His main accomplishment is swimming. He swam 1½ miles to the village this morning." In addition to being a good swimmer Dorothy became "a beautiful spring-board diver" and began winning competitions. (She carried this skill through to her 85th year.)

At this time, the favorite family vacations were spent at Lake Nojiri. Hot springs warmed the mountain lake and made it perfect for swimmers–an opportunity never lost on the Nelson children. On Sabbaths vacationing missionaries enjoyed rowing over to an island, a mile distant. There they had Sabbath School, church, and lunch together in privacy. During the winter Japanese friends charged only $4.00 to build a six-foot deep "ice cave" that lasted all summer. It provided "refrigeration" for the cabins, in spite of the fact that electricity operated only in the evenings. The packed snow could also be removed to churn ice cream.

When the twins returned to FEA, they left from their campus home in Naraha. When they returned home, it was to Tokyo. The summer of 1938 eighteen-year-old Richard spent hours at the Underwood typewriter preparing his father's doctoral dissertation. Four copies (with carbon paper) at a time. Not even one erasure was allowed. Work on his father's meticulous notes and highly technical research occupied him until he shipped home to start his freshman year at Walla Walla College. "I'm thinking about doing pre-med," he told his parents.

In November 1938, Andrew revisited the Naraha campus. This time he was a guest in the house where he and Vera had spent ten of their happiest years, growing up with the three children, the cats, and all. What a nostalgic journey! How dearly he loved the place! Back again among his beloved pine forests, he made a new discovery. One night he spoke to the "Naraha boys" on "Faith and Prayer." Right there a new awareness of the power of prayer came to him. "By being always right with God," he declared, "[I can] always be at ease spiritually."

By this time the long-lasting Japanese war in China had markedly worsened. Because of the fighting around Shanghai, FEA could not open in the fall. A few weeks later, however, the news came that the school would open in Kowloon, across the bay from Hong Kong. A British colony should ensure safety. The Nelson twins couldn't stop jumping up and down. After an exciting boat ride to Hong Kong, they and the other students were lodged in an old Chinese mansion there, and, once again, Far Eastern Academy opened.

At first, the pond in the landscaped garden seemed to be a lovely asset. Then students, including Dorothy, came down with malaria. With a lavish distribution of atabrin and plasma cream, the youngsters recovered. The teachers, however, had had enough. In the middle of the next school year they all moved back to Shanghai, since the Japanese had departed. Whatever the inconvenience, the FEA-ites thoroughly enjoyed being on the boat together again, bound northward. Such was the loyalty of all FEA students, the twins grieved deeply when the day came that their beloved school closed.

Then came a day in March, 1939. As he dug into his mail, Andrew Nelson found a plain Manila envelope from the University of Washington. It contained his PhD degree that had been issued on December 14, 1938. He leaned back, relaxed. Now, at age forty-four, he'd finished his formal education. Although he deeply appreciated the mentorship of his advisor, Dr. Pollard, from now on he could plan his own study, "do my own research and map out my own conclusions." No longer would his thinking be hampered by professors who believed that evolution is "another Bible."

From time to time, Andrew had used the knowledge gleaned from his research on the religions of Japan to good purpose. One day on the train, for instance, he talked to "an inquisitive old gentleman" about Christianity. His ability to speak about Shinto and Buddhism certainly attracted the man's attention. "It's a long task to win a Japanese to the Truth," Andrew admitted, "but . . . [I've] met a lot of splendid people, some of them from the very best families. I hope that the seed sown will bear fruit in some way or other."

Was the title of "Dr. Nelson" going to go to his head? Not after he had prayed for humility and had given thanks that this great task could now be safely removed from his prayer list. Still, there was room left for *some* pride. The university people wrote that the "typing job was the best one they'd ever received." That meant Number One Son Richard. Andrew smiled to himself. (Besides, news had now reached Tokyo that in the incoming freshman class of 300 at Walla Walla College, Richard had ranked seventh in the entrance tests.

Then, that evening, sweet-little-sixteen Dorothy looked up at him and said, "Daddy, I didn't know you knew so much!" Andrew had to smile again. Why not?

[1] In many countries where government examinations are the norm, rote memory work has been common. The teacher simply chooses the topic and the pupils memorize and repeat the set answers.
[2] A.N. Nelson, "Mighty Opportunities for Students at Japan Junior College," *Far Eastern Division Outlook* (September, 1936), pp. 4-5.
[3] *Far Eastern Division Outlook* (September, 1936), p. 8.
[4] Because of worsening political conditions the Far Eastern Division offices moved from Shanghai to Singapore in 1936. *China Division Reporter* (February, 1937), p. 8. Far Eastern Academy also transferred to Singapore a few months later.

12. War Clouds over Asia

In 1940, Richard Nelson settled into his first year of pre-med studies at Walla Walla, and the twins were happily absorbed in Grade 12 at Far Eastern Academy in Shanghai. In contrast, back at home in Tokyo, peculiar events were evolving.

Nine years later, in 1949, George Orwell would coin the phrase "thought police" in his anti-utopian novel, *Nineteen-Eighty-four*.[1] In Japan back in the 1930s these same people went by the title "Special Higher Police." The Imperial government had to know what dangerous thoughts might be lurking in the minds of citizens and foreigners alike. Charged with controlling speech, action, and thoughts, the thought police intimidated and harassed people night and day.[2] From 1928 onward, an estimated 60,000 people were arrested.[3]

Andrew first encountered this hostile force while he was principal of Japan Missionary College out in rural Chiba Prefecture. On the trains he frugally traveled 3rd-class. One day, a thought control officer accosted him. "He took me to 1st-class," Nelson remembered "to check my thoughts." Particularly he wanted to know what Andrew thought about the Sino-Japanese War that was still going on.[4]

Nelson gave what he and his colleagues had agreed would be their standard reply: "We know only what we read in the newspapers." Without further ceremony the policeman sent him back to his 3rd-class seat. Japanese citizens and foreigners alike had to figure out how to survive among the Thought Control Police.

Meanwhile, as principal of Japan Missionary College, Francis Millard had come under huge pressure to use textbooks that glorified the military regime. The authorities also urged him to take the students to worship at Shinto shrines. The Publishing House began struggling to know what to do with the Christian books in their stockroom. Although the literature work in Japan had begun in 1898, government regulations severely restricted what could be printed. The publication, *Toki no Shirish* (Signs of the Times), was confined to thirty-two pages.[5]

Upon taking up the presidency of the Japan Union Mission, Nelson found even more difficulty in dealing with the Bureau of Religions. Absolutely no concept of religious liberty existed there. One day, the chief officer told him: "Mr. Nelson, I fear there is no hope for your church here."

In a very short time Nelson knew the answer, for sure. At his office at mission headquarters he received a strange message from the Minister of Religious Affairs: "Your Seventh-day Adventist denomination is too small to be recognized in Japan. You can have official status only if you join up with some other small denominations."

Andrew's reply was unequivocal. "Since it is against the policy of our church to make such a merger, we must decline your offer."

"Therefore, your denomination can no longer be recognized in Japan." End of discussion. Nelson understood very well how to interpret these happenings. The government intended to eliminate the Seventh-day Adventist Church and then confiscate all of their properties.

Then the bombing of Pearl Harbor catapulted the United States into World War II, on the morning of December 7, 1941, one flaming, hot question erupted in America. "Why did they do that? Why does Japan act like that?" Few of the surprised Westerners had seen it coming.

Could there be any explanation for these alarming trends? In fact, there was. Long before that tragedy occurred, however, Andrew Nelson had carefully considered the matter. Indeed, he had some definite viewpoints.

To begin with, the Japanese had at least five very admirable characteristics that made working among them a real joy. First, they were extremely honest. He and many others could testify to having lost purses and other valuables, only to retrieve them days later from the police, perfectly in tact. Equally admirable was their immaculate cleanliness. Third, they believed in precision. You could set your watch by the time their trains left the station. Fourth, they were uniformly courteous, under all circumstances. Their lovely gardens bespoke their passionate love of beauty. Finally, they loved freedom. Andrew recalled the early years when "we enjoyed freedom to travel, teach, preach, and to think. . . . We even had freedom from robbers."

"How then," someone will ask, "does that harmonize with

Japan's many acts of violence? The theft of Manchuria (1931) the pillage of China and the rape of Nanking (1937), the treachery of Pearl Harbor (1941), destruction of Corregidor, the terror of the Bataan Death March (1942), and much, much more."

According to Nelson, we can readily trace the connection. When Japan stepped out of feudalism, the United States virtually adopted the budding nation. Democracy, education, industry, commerce, medicine, religious and civil liberty—all of it became available to the common people. The climax of Americanization came in the rehabilitation after the Great Tokyo Earthquake in 1923.

Still, one circumstance remained. Although officially open to Western influence and trade Japan was still a shogunate. Therefore, the history of the Three Shogunates[6] needs to be understood.

When the central government of Japan fell into decline in 784 AD, the Divine Emperor moved his court from Nara to Kyoto. Art and literature flourished in the new capital for the next 400 years. The *daimyo* (the provincial *samurai* clan lords), however, held the real power, and they pulled away from the control of the Emperor. Feuding among the warrior clans continued until 1185 when the emperor appointed the first *shogun* (military commander) from the victorious *samurai* factions. Thus, Minamoto Yoritomo would set the pace for military dictatorship for the next 700 years.

Therefore, when the Japanese threw their country into World War II, astonished Westerners cried: "Imagine them doing a terrible thing like that!" Even the briefest knowledge of Japanese history, however, could have answered that question.

The Shoguns of Japan

1. **The Kamakura Shogunate** (1185-1336). The first shogun, Minomoto, set up his military government at the coastal village of Kamakura. Two invasions by China's Mongol Emperor Kublai Khan weakened this stronghold.

2. **The Ashikaga Shogunate** (1336-1568). A *samurai* general, Ashigawa Takauji, made Kyoto his seat of power. Here the refinements and ceremonies of Zen Buddhism were practiced. Outside, however, civil disorder prevailed as the clan lords contended for land and power.

3. **The Tokugawa Shogunate** (1603-1867). The powerful Tokugawa clan fought its way to the top of *samurai* society. Out of a population of about thirty million, only about two million Japanese belonged to the elite *samurai* group. They despised Western culture and isolated Japan for over 200 years. They imposed strong class lines and demanded rigid conformity to customs.[7] (Otherwise instant and very harsh punishment followed.)

Samurai society lived by a strict code of behavior that has been compared to the traditions of chivalry in feudal Europe.

Bushido: The Samurai Warrior Code

1. Unquestioning loyalty and respect to the feudal lord.
2. Development of military skills and fearlessness in battle.
3. Self-discipline and self-control.
4. Disregard of material wealth, disdain of money.
5. Rejection of soft living, indifference to suffering and discomfort.
6. Contempt for surrender to the enemy, defeat shameful.
7. Complete devotion to the Emperor.
8. Honor of parents.
9. Personal honor valued above life itself.
10. Honesty.
11. Compassion, generosity.
12. Politeness.

Against this background it is easy to see why a Japanese soldier could not endure the extreme dishonor of capture or imprisonment. This would be a colossal "loss of face." Under the Code of Bushido a Japanese warrior didn't actually mind dying. He would, however, perform it ritually by *seppuku* (or *hara-kiri*). That is, the extremely painful disemboweling with his sword. Faced with execution he favored beheading. Or the firing squad. He perceived hanging as the ultimate insult to his honor.

Finally, by 1867, Japan came under pressure to modernize itself. Many began to question the legitimacy of the *samurais'* fierce hold on the government. After two hundred years in the social "strait jacket" imposed by Tokugawa, the shogunate ended. Supreme power would eventually return to the Emperor.

At the same time, foreign powers were trying to get into Japan, beginning with Commodore Perry's arrival in 1853. The issue of foreign relations spawned crippling internal conflict. What Japan needed was unification. To this end, the young Emperor Meiji Mutsuhito moved his court to Yedo (Tokyo) in 1867 and occupied the great Tokugawa castle there. Four years later, he completed his reforms. Abolishing both feudalism and the clans, he defined three classes: (1) Nobles and former *daimyo* lords (*kazoku*); (2) Former *samurai* (*shizoku*), and (3) The commoners (*heimin*).

Next, Emperor Meiji plunged into technological and industrial development. This left *the samurai* craving a war to fight. Although they regretted the loss of their privileged position, they scorned turning to commerce, even though they still had permission to carry their two swords (one for battle and one for *seppuku*/suicide). Preferring a life of war rather than peace, the disgruntled *samurai* thus provided a "reservoir" of militarism. It would feed into Japan's aggressions in East Asia, and would eventually lead to Pearl Harbor.[8]

Unfortunately, Japanese Imperial education had been modeled on the authoritarian Prussian plan, forming a link for future liaison with Nazi Germany. It promoted national unification and worship of the Emperor, obedient and respectful students, high literacy, knowledge of science, and traditional morality. Conspicuously absent, however, was freedom of thought and conscience.

The Nazi Party, of course, was all too willing to foster Japan's escalating military ambition. As early as 1901 that Japanese secret society of "Black Dragons"[9] made its money off the Chinese opium trade and had international influence. This ultra-nationalistic organization came to the attention of the German linguist, Dr. Karl Haushofer who found the ideals of the *samurai bushido* highly compatible with "the Teutonic spirit." He and Herman Hess met with the Japanese attaché, Matsuoko, in 1934. Together they concluded that Germany and Japan could, indeed, be comfortable as allies.

Concurrently, Japan had re-established the ancient Shinto religion. Now the Emperor would be worshipped as a descendant of the sun goddess, Amaterasu. He would appear all-powerful, but his advisers made sure that the real power stayed with them. The Emperor had, in fact, one of the longest genealogical lines in the world. He was directly descended from Emperor Jimmu who ruled about the time of Christ.

Hoping to pacify those demanding democracy, Japan voted in its first Constitution in 1889. Nonetheless, the old policies would die hard. Indeed, the perpetrators of the Pacific War (1941-1945) actually created Japan's Fourth Shogunate (1937-1945). By 1939 Japan had aligned itself with the Axis powers, sympathetic to Hitler's raging war that had broken out in Europe.

[1] George Orwell, *Nineteen Eighty-four* (London:Secker and Warburg Publishing, 1949).
[2] *Time,* "Japan: Thought Control." http://www.time.com/time/magazine/article/0,9171,788588,00.html (October 2010).
[3] *Time,* "Japan: Thought Control." http://www.time.com/time/magazine/article/0,9171,788588,00.html (October 2010).
[4] The Qing Dynasty of China and Meiji Japan fought the First Sino-Japanese War (1894-1895) over control of Korea, a tributary of China. Victorious Japan lost 240,000 men, but China lost 630,000. The Second Sino-Japanese War (1937-1945) was being waged over the Chinese mainland. In 1932 Japan occupied Manchuria, setting up the puppet state of Manchukuo. The attack on Pearl Harbor merged this conflict with World War II.
[7] The hierarchical classes in the Japanese shogunates were as follows: The Emperor, the *samurai,* rice farmers, craftsmen, artisans, fishermen, and merchants. (The *samurai* despised the merchants). Still further down followed: the entertainers, leather workers, beggars and executioners. Moving from one class to another in feudal Japanese society was virtually impossible.
[8] See "Last Secrets of the Axis." Military History Channel TV (June 26, 2010). A master-spy, Dr. Bernard Julius Otto Kuehn and his family moved to Honolulu in 1935. This German Nazi agent worked with the Japanese Consuluate there and ultimately watched the Pearl Harbor attack from his house. He was arrested by the FBI on February 21, 1942. In exchange for valuble information, his death sentence was commuted to hard labor.
[9] The "Black Dragon Society" was founded by Ryohei Uchida in 1901. Initially it dedicated itself to drive the Russian Empire out of East Asia.

13. Military Connections

In 1940 the Far Eastern Division Committee ordered all missionaries in Japan to evacuate. Some went to the Philippines, thought to be a secure place because of the long-standing American influence there. The Nelsons, however, transferred to Shanghai, China, where Andrew took charge of all of the Home Study Institutes in the Far Eastern Division, a job that called for a great deal of travel.[1] For the time being, at least, the twins could live at home and still attend their dearly loved Far Eastern Academy.

More importantly, Andrew was assigned to the leadership of the Language School. Clearly, a good choice, for he was already a recognized linguist.

He used the "direct method" of teaching whereby new missionaries learned Chinese with amazing speed and accuracy. As a young child learns by hearing the words repeated, the teacher spoke the Chinese words over and over. So the students copied what they heard. In fact, they were fined if they spoke English! Nelson provided the students with four Chinese language teachers—one each for vocabulary, reading, writing, and conversation.

Among the recently arrived missionaries (October 1940) were the Thomas Geratys (with infant son Larry). He had been appointed to be Education Secretary and school principal. Almost immediately their lives were torn to shreds. By retreating to the interior, Chungking (Chongqing) and Hankow, they, along with the Koch family, did not evacuate. The latter were from Germany, so they thought it safe to remain in Japan. Still, they had virtually no opportunity to do missionary work. The stories of how they all survived could not be known until the end of the war. A saga all of itself.

In that autumn of 1940 threats of war pressed in ominously upon the Shanghai office of the Far Eastern Division. Drastic measures

had to be taken. Whoever was due for furlough was urged to take it.
Soon afterwards the U. S. government sent ships to evacuate women
and children.

Vera and the twins returned to the U. S. on the *SS Washington*.
Back in California, she rented a house at Pacific Union College so that
Donald and Dorothy could finish their senior year at PUC Academy.
Not without grief, however. Dorothy was bitterly disappointed to
have missed graduating from FEA. Happily, her enjoyment of music
lessons somewhat abated her sorrow.

Meanwhile, only five people remained in the Shanghai office:
Andrew Nelson, Elder and Mrs. John Oss, Gertrude Green, and M. D.
Howard.   Soon it became impossible to comply with all of the new
regulations. Daily, Japanese planes flew low over the city.[2] Still on
task, Nelson labored to move the mission headquarters to Chung- king in
West China. Then another directive came from the General Conference:
"Come home immediately."

At virtually a moment's notice, he found a ship leaving
Shanghai. His passport, however, had expired.[3] When he rushed to
the U. S. Embassy, he must have set the world record for finding his
way through diplomatic bureaucracy and red tape. He had his new
passport in hand in just ten minutes!

Although America's involvement in the war appeared to be imminent, Andrew wouldn't simply "go home." He had business to set
in order before he departed. In fact, his "flight plan" called for several
stops. First, came Manchuria. He made his way through south Japan
and Korea and then crossed the Yalu River to arrive in Mukden.

The puppet government there was in the act of closing down
the Adventist school. By-passing the Chinese official, Andrew talked
to the real political power, the Japanese Vice-Mayor. The latter was
more than glad to find an American who could talk Japanese.

The problem had arisen from the fact that China, Korea, and
Japan all used the same ideographs (characters). These could carry
different meanings in each language. Thus, the Japanese word for
"to regulate" meant "to shut up" in Chinese. The document had been
written in Japanese and then read by Chinese. The school was, as it
turned out, to be inspected, not closed.

Nelson next conferred with Elder Kenneth H. Wood about
turning over the mission work to Chinese leadership. He also took a
sick missionary with him, and put him on an American-bound ship in

Kobe, Japan. By the time he reached Tokyo, Andrew had to help two more ailing workers to get out of the country.

Parting with his Japanese associates was a final and painful passage. Foreign workers staying in the country would end up in concentration camps. If the Japanese Christians gave any aid, they would be marked as traitors. As it was, when church property was confiscated by the government, the national workers (young and old) themselves went to prison. As if part of a dying body, one organ after another was shutting down in the Japan Mission.

Finally, Nelson himself boarded the *Tatsuta Maru* for her last trans-Pacific voyage. Upon arrival in San Francisco, Nelson delivered his two patients, rejoined his family, and attended the General Conference meetings then in session. At last, the family could settle down together at Pacific Union College to enjoy a much-needed third furlough.

The apparent tranquility, however, was an illusion and very short-lived. On the morning of December 7, 1941, his colleague, Ralph Watts, came bounding up the hill to the Nelson home yelling, "They're at it! The War is on!" He stopped in the doorway, breathless. "Pearl Harbor has been bombed, and our whole Pacific fleet has been sunk!"

In other words, the entire Far Eastern Division had just been swallowed up in the war.

Before his departure Nelson had done his best to provide for the church he was leaving behind. Anticipating hostilities he brought in a considerable amount of cash so that the Union officers could carry on, at least for a time.

He could not, however, forestall all suffering. At exactly 5:00 a.m., two months after December 7, a simultaneous arrest raid was made throughout Japan. Every Union official, pastor and every important layman was carried off to prison—all with very minimal legal process. They remained in prison until the end of the war. Although none were tortured, they were heavily interrogated *ad infinitum*. (One or two died in prison of natural causes.)

In their meticulous way, the Japanese government confiscated all bank accounts, the college and all other church properties. Then they carefully continued to pay salaries to the families from the monies they had confiscated. Amazingly enough, there is sometimes "honor among thieves."

Nonetheless, the great Pacific war was on. She didn't know it yet, but Japan had aroused the sleeping giant that was America. Mistakenly, the bombing of Pearl Harbor didn't bring the immediate collapse they'd anticipated. The aggressors somehow managed to ignore the new reality they'd created for themselves.

From that day forward, the Far Eastern Division missionaries were "farmed out" in various conferences and institutions. Nelson ended up as Academic Dean of Emmanuel Missionary College (now Andrews University). They bought a house near the college, and Andrew took up his duties as supervisor of summer school.

Actually, this appointment suited his scholarly mind very well. He enjoyed teaching an education class also. Many students hailed his classroom success: "We like him for his seeing and understanding the mind, not to mention his trait of thinking and doing. He's straightforward and fatherly, well grounded and backed by a life record of experiences, a friend to all."

Concurrently, the two Nelson boys were busy working out their own problems. Richard had been accepted into Loma Linda School of Medicine and was engaged to marry Carol Brewer the next summer. His request for army deferment, disappointingly, had been turned down.[4] (He had to postpone medicine and fighting the draft board.) Donald, on the other hand, had been accepted to Loma Linda—with an army commission to pay his way through medicine.

Before the Nelsons could settle into the real campus routine in Michigan, however, a puzzling series of letters began to arrive. Andrew ignored the first two summonses from the U. S. government. When the third arrived, he inquired of the General Conference administrators, "What shall I do?"

The reply was clear and simple: "Honor your country."

Even with his extensive experience in Japan, Andrew Nelson could hardly foresee the part he would play in progress of the war, to say nothing of reconstructing the peace afterwards.

[1] Andrew Nelson purchased the Scharffenberg personal library for the Home Study Institute. Very efficiently he posted a request for all borrowed books to be returned. *China Division Reporter* (September 15,1940), p. 8; (December, 1940), p. 8.

[2] Andrew Nelson and M. E. Loewen described 300 bombings in Chungking, China. They reported to an informal faculty reception at Pacific Union College that hosted sixty-three "refugee" missionaries in the area. *Pacific Union Recorder* (December, 1941). p. 2.

[3] On April 10, 1940, the U. S. government had cancelled all American passports as a wartime precaution.

[4] Richard Nelson could not begin his medical degree at Loma Linda until after he was discharged from the Army. He took a residency in General Surgery and became certified by American Board of Surgery. He has practiced medicine in Corona, California, for the past forty years. He is also the only Caucasian to hold a lifetime Japanese Medical License.

14. The Intelligence Exchange

Japan's Third Shogunate had collapsed some eighty years earlier. Therefore, the Western Allies were utterly mystified when they faced the battle-hardened, Emperor-worshipping, Bushido-consecrated Japanese in the World War II. Likewise the terrain baffled them. They fought in a maze of islands. Thousands of them. Some no larger than Central Park in New York.

The reprehensible General Hideki Tojo (1884-1948) turned out to be one of the main villains in that sorrowful drama. Publicly and abundantly he embodied the old *samurai* attitudes, becoming the ruling "shogun" in Japan's war machine. He and his military clique had been pushing Japan toward World War II since the 1930s. As Prime Minister (1941-1944) and supreme military commander he completely controlled his country's affairs. Indeed, he was the primary architect and advocate of Japan's going to war with the United States. As the Imperial Army moved from victory to victory, Tojo enjoyed great popularity. Of course, he much admired Nazi Germany.

Because the people had great respect for their Emperor, the militarists always prefaced their announcements with "Hirohito says . . ." Yet he had little power.[1]

Consequently America was in dire straits and totally unprepared for the challenges of the Pearl Harbor attack. It was discovered that in the whole world there were only sixty Americans who could handle the Japanese language fluently. Ten percent of these were Seventh-day Adventist missionaries. (Unfortunately, businessmen and other "colonial types" in Japan hadn't bothered themselves to learn the language.)

Andrew suddenly found his linguistic talents to be top priority. Now almost fifty years old he was well past the draft age. Nonetheless, the War Department assured him that if he had any difficulty resigning from his job with the College, they had "ways of getting him."

Counseling with the brethren at the General Conference, he accepted the advice of E. L. Branson, then a Vice-President. "We've always been asking the government for help for our boys in the army. Now the tables are turned, and Uncle Sam calls on us for help. I think you'd better go."

Hastily a leave-of-absence was arranged with Emmanuel Missionary College. Three weeks after Pearl Harbor, Andrew and Vera moved to Washington, leaving their new house in Michigan to their children.

Andrew Nelson entered the U. S. Army as a (Civilian) Research Specialist, with the rank equivalent to Colonel. He would serve for almost four years. In his new work he found very compatible office mates who had been called up for the same reason that he had—fluency in the Japanese language. These men were his former fellow workers, Benjamin Hoffman, Clarence Thurston, and Francis Millard. They discovered that all available reference materials in Japanese were woefully deficient and very much outdated.

Twenty-three years earlier when he first arrived in Japan Nelson had thrown himself into the mastering of the Japanese language. At first, the skill served as an aid to his teaching at Japan Junior College and as a convenience in his ministry in the Mission. He could not have foreseen, however, that his gift for languages would change the course of his life. In fact, it would make a huge contribution to the winning of the War in the Pacific. The work of the bright minds of these linguists would ultimately save tens of thousands of American lives.

Gradually Andrew prepared a set of Japanese-English military dictionaries, sponsored by both the Americans and the British. They were reproduced and widely used by both the Army and Navy. One of them was the *150,000 Japanese-English Technical Terms Dictionary*. Later, having become a very skilled lexicographer, Nelson authored *The Original Modern Reader's Japanese-English Character Dictionary*.[2] Even today, this volume remains the most comprehensive dictionary of its kind and is a classical resource work.

When asked to suggest another name to join the Intelligence Department, Nelson suggested his older son Richard. At the time the young man was in the induction center in Monterey, California, unable to proceed with his plans to go to medical school. No complaints, however, when he found himself in Washington D. C. working with his father and sharing in the curious hybrid status of being "a civilian in military capacity." He and his bride Carol lived with his parents. Each work day father and son used to go off to work together on a motorcycle.

As a Lieutenant in the Signal Corps, Richard worked with Al Dwyer to reconstruct the Japanese Army Shipping Code. They succeeded well, especially in the matter of tracing ship movements, oil production and so forth. In order to have Sabbaths off, Richard worked every Saturday night. He spent many hours scanning diplomatic traffic between Tokyo and Berlin.

Finally, Nelson and Dwyer broke the Japanese Code. The Japanese were sly enemies, and the jungle encounters were often costly. Oddly enough, the Japanese never changed the Code throughout the war. Occasionally, they'd insert an item intended to confuse.[3] Nonetheless, however scrambled their operations appeared to be, the young code-breakers in the U. S. Intelligence Department still accurately tracked all of their comings and goings. They knew exactly where all of the Japanese ships were going and which planes would fly officers to certain places.

The assassination of Isoroku Yamamoto (1884-1943) was a case in point. The death of the Commander-in-Chief of the Imperial Japanese Navy was, as planned, a psychological blow. When it was known that Yamamoto would be arriving at the airfield in Bouganville from Rabaul (in the Solomon Islands) at 9:35 a.m. on April 18, 1943, a squadron of P-38 Lightning aircraft flew over 400 miles to bring down the Admiral's plane.[4]

Because the Japanese rapidly defeated large portions of the Far East immediately after Pearl Harbor, they actually weakened themselves. The War Department knew just where to sever their "lifelines." To do this, they knew exactly where to intercept the warships and cut them off from their homeland.

In 1945 the Pacific War began to wind down toward an American victory. One day while walking along Carroll Avenue in Takoma Park, Andrew Nelson met Elder Charles Longacre (1871-1958), the veteran religious liberty man of the Seventh-day Adventist Church. Andrew, of course never missed a beat when it came to affairs in the Orient

"Elder Longacre!" Nelson accosted the old man in mid-step. "When the peace negotiations get under way, you need to get someone over to Japan just as fast as you can. We need to get Shinto disestablished as the State Religion and restore religious liberty."

Because Japanese nationalism had taken such an ominous turn to militarism, post-war reconstruction now had to establish religious liberty in the defeated nation. Little did Andrew know that he would be one of the officers appointed to do the job.

After hostilities ended, General MacArthur chose men from the Intelligence Department to join him in Japan and to help set up the new government. Unfortunately, Hoffman and Thurston had died, but Millard and Nelson were available to go. As civilian researchers they could have left the army. Keen to get back to the Far East, however, they joined MacArthur's forces in Japan.

Andrew was appointed to assist Commander Bunce, General MacArthur's "decree-writer." As a specialist in religion, he and Nelson instantly formed a very compatible team. The document that they would prepare would disestablish Shinto and end religious persecution in Japan. (Now Andrew realized the full implications of the choice he had made for his doctoral research years earlier, "The Religions of Japan.")

On the trans-Pacific flight their refueling stop in Guam had far-reaching influence. The name "Adventist" was wholly unknown there because all previous attempts to evangelize the island had failed. At the time, a group of Seventh-day Adventist servicemen was stationed in Guam. On weekends they gathered in the chapel of the 204th General Hospital.[5]

Because of the efforts of Pharmacists Mate 1st-class, Henry Metzker, nine members of the prominent local Ullao family requested baptism. Although the Far Eastern Division had promised to send in a Filipino pastor, the war was not entirely over. No one could tell how long the wait might be.

"I'm so glad you're in Guam." Young Metzker shook hands with Nelson and Millard. "You'll be here a few days."

"Oh no!" Andrew countered. "We have to go right on with this plane. At best, we have only an hour or two. We've been ordered directly to Tokyo. I'm sorry . . . "

"I have nine Guamanians I've been studying with, and they're ready for baptism." Metzger looked at them mildly. "No, you're going to stay several days and baptize this earnest family. You'll be interested to know that they're descendants of a former Spanish governor."

Speechless, Nelson and Millard stared at the young soldier. "But how . . . ?"

"We've been praying," Metzker went on. "I expect you'll be here about a week."

Within an hour the answer to prayer blew in in the form of a typhoon. All aircraft were grounded for six days. During that time, the Ulloa family was baptized in the clear waters of Tuman Bay. Then, "at leisure," the two visitors fellowshipped with the Adventist GI's on base.

Thus the Seventh-day Adventist Church was planted in Guam. In subsequent years American and Filipino missionaries built up a strong presence on that North Pacific island.

Perhaps one of the most efficient generals the United States ever produced, MacArthur consulted with other Allied officers in Australia. Together they formulated the plan for cutting the Japanese "life line." Although they didn't realize it at the time, after Pearl Harbor, Japan spread themselves "too thin" in the vast range of Pacific Islands.

By mid-June, 1945, the Allied forces had mastered the vast distances and overcome the Japanese troops. After the eighty-two-day-long Battle of Okinawa they stood on the very threshold of Japan itself. Invasion of Kyushu and occupation of all of the islands appeared the next obvious step with potentially heavy casualties. The final victory over Japan, however, came suddenly. After six months of incendiary fire-bombing, the two atomic bombs effectively concluded the dispute.

According to Andrew Nelson, however, the second A bomb might never have been needed. Already in 1944 the U.S. bombing of Japan became so severe that Emperor Hirohito became alarmed. The houses built of wood and paper exploded in flames on all sides. Dressed in civilian clothes he walked the Tokyo streets incognito. The destruction was even worse than he imagined. This event occurred six months before the A bombs.

Back in his house within the palace, the Emperor prepared a message of surrender. He called for the four years of fighting to end, lest they had to face "The obliteration of the race [and] the extinction of human civilization." Instead of dispatching it directly to the United States, however, he sent it by way of Russia. No response. Scheming and lethargic, Russia never passed the message on.[6] She was just waiting for the most advantageous time to declare war on Japan

Hirohito decided to resend the surrender message through Switzerland and Sweden, employing his friend Prime Minister Suzuki.[7] Summoning the Supreme Council, he said: "My decision to accept the Potsdam Declaration was not made lightly." Unless the war was terminated Japan's "national polity" would be destroyed and the people "ruined." He demanded that all present should agree to his "Imperial Rescript."

At 11 p.m. the Emperor finished recording, and a messenger

stood by ready to take the message to Radio Tokyo for broadcast to the nation. Two chiefs of staff and the War Minister, however, were violently opposed to the idea of surrender. About 1,000 dissident soldiers infiltrated the palace compound. They tried to invade the Emperor's house and steal the Imperial Rescript. Fearing assassination Hirohito and others went into hiding.

More favorable to the Emperor than the militarists, the radio station made a copy of the Emperor's surrender message. The insurgents seized the first one but the copy remained hidden in a safe. Ultimately it proved what the Emperor's intentions had been six months before the end of the Pacific War. There was only one radio station, and people had to have it turned on continuously, expecting an American invasion at any moment.

The A bombs had just been dropped. Richard Nelson was working his graveyard shift in the Intelligence Department. Suddenly, he gasped, "Why that's the surrender message!"

He listened carefully: "There is no hope of winning the war, and to avoid more suffering of my people, contact the Allies and sue for peace at any cost."

Richard phoned his supervisor. "It has come through," he almost choked on his excitement. "The good news at last."

"I can't believe it," Colonel Aurel exclaimed. "Are you sure?"

"Well, come over and see it for yourself."

At 3 a.m. the supervisor arrived. Richard translated it, checked with the Colonel, and then sent it on to President Truman. By then it was about 4 a.m.

If Emperor Hirohito had not trusted Russia with his first surrender message, no A bombs would have fallen. History could have been written very differently.

Instead, the Emperor's stony-faced Japanese delegation of sixteen officers attended the preparation of the surrender documents on August 19. In their beribboned gray-green uniforms and peaked caps—*samurai* swords at their sides—they made a pathetic picture at the Manila Conference. After two days of discussion with the linguists hard at work they carried away the surrender documents, meticulously translated into perfect Japanese.

On September 2, 1945, the Japanese delegates met with the Allied officers aboard the U. S. battleship *Missouri*, afloat in Tokyo

Bay. Swarms of smaller vessels formed a tight circle around the great warship while army and navy planes hovered overhead. Signing the official surrender document took about twenty minutes.

WAR DEPARTMENT
Commendation to Dr. Andrew N. Nelson

For meritorious civilian service and
outstanding performance of duty.
For initiative in undertaking lexicographical projects designed to
effect great saving of time for government agencies
For his brilliant organization and unflagging devotion to duty,
and
For his readiness to forget self in order to
put his talents at the service of others.

26 February, 1946

---

[1] In almost any documentation it is noted that any Japanese Royal was taken from their family to be brought up in the military tradition.
[2] Andrew Nelson's Dictionary contains 5,000 characters, 70,000 compounds, and 10,000 current readings, along with concise English definitions. (1112 pages). It was computerized in 2008.
[3] The Japanese never penetrated the American Code because it utilized the very difficult Navajo language, used in battlefield communications.
[4] See en.wikipedia.org/wiki/Isoroku-Yamamoto#Death. (October 2010).
[5] V. T. Armstrong, "Report on Far Eastern Division," *Review and Herald*. (June 13,1946), p. 157. (http://www.adventistarchives.org/doc_info.asp?DocID=93097), (October 2010) [archive].
[6] Instead of transmitting the Emperor's surrender message, Russia took time to acquire more territory. In fact, she never declared war on Japan until after the A bombs had dropped on Hiroshima (August 6) and Nagasaki (August 9).
[7] The seventy-seven-year-old Suzuki was an avowed pacifist, and his presence signaled Japan's desire for peace. In 1936 he had been caught in the middle of an uprising of young militarists. Although he was shot and left for dead, he survived. In the riot of 1944, his house was burned to the ground.

15. Picking Up the Pieces

On August 15, 1945, President Harry Truman announced that Japan had accepted the terms of surrender. Dropping the atom bomb shaped the way in which the war ended. That happening became a huge center of interest, an odd mix of confused fear mingled with a hopeful awe. The result would be the birth of Japan's policy of religious freedom, an event in which Andrew Nelson would play an enthusiastic part.

With the Japanese forces widely scattered and with communications seriously disrupted, getting the surrender message out was difficult. In fact, some Japanese soldiers in the remote jungles of South East Asia would not know that the war was over for years to come. Nor would they realize that their Emperor had officially abandoned his "divinity."[1]

When Hirohito made his unprecedented nation-wide radio broadcast to inform his country that they had suffered their first military defeat, few people had even heard his voice before.

General MacArthur had a rehabilitation strategy to help Japan get back on its feet, one that he hoped would prevent the usual chaos that follows a military defeat. With the samurai-type militarists defeated, the General went back to Japan's leaders from a more peaceful time. Obviously he needed good translators to communicate with Japan's new government. Therefore, just one month after the end of the war, the U. S. government sent Andrew Nelson, Francis Millard, and Richard Nelson (young as he was) to post-war Japan for this purpose. They worked in the Civil Information and Education Sections of the American Headquarters in Tokyo.

While Nelson and Millard served as interpreters for the army officers, they had their evenings and Sabbaths free to hunt for the Adventist church leaders and to help reorganize the Japan Union

Mission. Even before they arrived, however, a large group of Adventist GI's had already "gotten things going." Everyone rejoiced together in "wonderful prayer meetings" on the newly revived Amanuma compound.[2]

The visitors were appalled by the devastation of Tokyo—and then amazed that the fires had burned up to the walls of the mission compound and stopped. Their meetings with the church members were highly emotional. They wept as they heard the testimony of those who had faced imprisonment and cruel torture. "We held their hands," Millard recalled. "We saw in each face a martyr's testimony."[3]

Pastor Eikichi Seino, Superintendent of the Kyushu Mission, vividly described how Japanese Seventh-day Adventists had endured the war years.[4] Baptized in 1907 and first becoming a colporteur, he was ordained in 1927. In 1941 the Peace Preservation Law of Japan dictated that anyone "undermining the national polity" or "impairing the prestige of the shrines of the Imperial House [Shinto]" would be imprisoned for a year or more. Dying for the Emperor *Yamato Damashi* (Japan Spirit) was the highest good. This system resulted, however, in a total loss of freedom. Since all citizens were obligated to the Shinto gods for victory in war, disobedience immediately marked one as a traitor.

With the churches closed, the members scattered into the countryside, though not necessarily to safety. Wholesale arrests of Adventists occurred, and they were mercilessly oppressed. Refusal to engage in shrine worship brought social ostracism, constant ridicule, and much worse. On the Monday morning of September 20, 1943, the entire Seventh-day Adventist church came "under investigation."

Seino was thrown into a cell with burglars, swindlers, and murderers. The place was alive with fleas, lice, bedbugs and horrific odors. In the first 121 days he endured fifty-three interrogations, plus daily beatings. The next prison term lasted for 226 days. The Thought Control Police repeatedly asked, "What orders do you get from America?" The only food he had was what friends and family brought to him. They were also endangered because Christianity was viewed as "American."

In MacArthur's Occupation Government Andrew Nelson was appointed head of the "Religious Section" (Religious Research Analyst). Because of his doctoral research ten years earlier, he was well qualified to write the religious freedom portion. This job put him in a good position to work on the return of church properties to their rightful owners. Remembering the 1940 dictum by the Minister of Religious Affairs that the Seventh-day Adventist church could never be recognized in Japan, Andrew took great pleasure in writing the "religious freedom" clause that went into the new Japanese constitution. He even had the opportunity to speak with the former minister and to remind him that, indeed, "the tables had turned."

When the mythological Shinto Cult ceased to be the state religion, the Japanese glorification of war could be much diminished. Tensions centered on the Yasukuni Shrine in Tokyo, founded by Emperor Meiji in 1869. This temple contained the ashes and was dedicated to all who had given their lives for the Emperor. Today the *kami* (spirit-souls) number 2,466,000, all of whom, we are told, share the one available seat!

Fortunately, the new Shinto Directive at the end of the war separated Church and State. With all of the connections with Japanese Imperialism severed, Yasukuni became an exclusively religious shrine. An estimated 90 % of its adherents fell away. Nelson considered this event to be the greatest missionary opportunity Christianity had ever had in Japan.

The democratization of Japan, Nelson wrote confidently would make it "a different country from now on." The "freedom to preach" without police present was the new reality. Indeed, it was all coming up for the first free election in Japan since 1936 when the militarists got control of the Cabinet. "The Japanese are ready to listen to Christianity as never before. . . . They are particularly ready to hear us because of the definite message we bear." When he conducted a baptism of twenty-six people in Yokohama, Andrew found among them the daughter of the former Chief of the Thought-Control police in that city. Moreover, two of the same man's sons were set to attend the newly re-opened Japan Missionary College."[5]

Japan's new constitution also dictated that Japan would have no army, navy, or air force. The destruction of existing weapons and ammunition now released money to create a higher standard of living than this new "nation of peace" had ever known.

Exuberant over the ending of the Pacific War, thousands of military personnel were more than eager to get home for Christmas. Caught up among them was Lt. Richard Nelson, detained in Tokyo until December. His wife Carol was about to deliver their first baby.

He got as far as Seattle and stayed with his Uncle Reuben Nelson. Although he talked to Carol on the phone, there was no way he could get home to Virginia. Every seat on every known mode of transportation was booked up. He took the matter as philosophically as possible. When Baby Carol Rae arrived on December 18, 1945, Richard sent his wife a telegram couched in the best military terms: "Congratulations. It was more important for me to be at the laying of the keel than for the launching."

Meanwhile, certain excitable American evangelists (Some Seventh-day Adventists among them) had been announcing that Japan would lead the "Kings of the East" into the Battle of Armageddon. Nelson's combination of army experience, his intellectual pursuits, and his commitment to the Christian gospel qualified him to comment on these interpretations of prophecy that had cropped up toward the end of World War II. He had no patience with this kind of dogmatism and mishandling of prophecy. "Today Japan lies prostrate at the feet of the victors. Daily we are destroying tons of explosives, planes, and weapons of war." The very idea of this kind of sensationalism, he declared, is "out of place." Indeed, he found it a nuisance and altogether "ridiculous."[6]

The reconstruction of mission work was an enormous undertaking. The Far Eastern Division was the only part of the world church of Seventh-day Adventists that was completely overrun by World War II. It lost five Union missions along with all of their institutions. In March of 1941 all church leadership had been turned over to the nationals.[7] No neutral area remained where a foreign missionary could work. Moreover, the foreigners had to be evacuated to protect, as far as possible, the lives of the national believers. Either they went home or faced internment camp and/or death

At the General Conference Session in 1946 one of the hottest items on the agenda was how to put the Far Eastern Division back together again. The many missionaries who had left as refugees and even those who survived the Japanese concentration camps were more than ready to return to their work.[8]

While some people can never adjust to living and working in a foreign country, others simply cannot be stopped. Early in 1945, Andrew Nelson already voiced the heady rush of excitement as World War II finally ended and the mission fields opened up once more.[9] "Yes, soon we shall be going back!" he wrote. The zeal to go again, coupled with enthusiastic fund-raising, was absolutely intoxicating. "Some of us are going to have the privilege of going back to the mission-fields from which we were recalled because of the war; some of us will be sending our children out as missionaries; and all of us are going to have a part in engaging in this grand post-war foreign mission program."

Typical of the surge of interest in renewed mission activity was the weekend in October 1945, when both Andrew Nelson and Francis Millard visited the Pacific Union College campus. Almost like two schoolboys, they spoke enthusiastically about Japan and the prospects of renewed missionary effort there.[10]

Institutions and homes lay in ruins, yes. "But," Andrew declared, "soon we shall be going back!" There were other post-war mission-field projects around the world, of course. For those who had lived and worked in that "fascinating group of peninsulas and islands which constitute the far-flung Far Eastern Division," however, the intense loyalty became universal.[11]

Missionaries returning to the Far East went out by the hundreds. Division president, V. T. Armstrong characterized the moves not just as geographical. "We needed spiritual rehabilitation also," he added.[12]

It took about a year to get the Japan Missionary College and the Tokyo hospital going again. Francis Millard became the Union President.

For Andrew and Vera Nelson, however, other plans had been made.

[1] As late as 1973 one Japanese soldier was found living in a cave near the village of Talofofo where Jerry and Mitzi Wiggle worked at the time. He had survived by raiding people's gardens. But he'd never betrayed his Emperor.

[2] Andrew Nelson, cover letter to *The Ministry*. Eikichi Seino, "Wartime Persecution in Japan," translated by Andrew Nelson, *Australasian Record* (October 7, 1948), p. 3.

[3] W. P. Bradley and V. T. Armstrong, "An Evening with the Far Eastern Division." General Conference Report # 10. *Review and Herald* (June 20, 1946), pp. 227-229.

[4] Eickichi Seino, "Wartime Persecution in Japan," translated by Andrew Nelson. *Australasian Record* (October 7, 1946), pp. 3, 6.

[5] General Conference Report, *Australasian Record* (September 9, 1946), pp. 7-8.

[6] Andrew Nelson, "Japan and the Kings of the East," *The Ministry* (June, 1946), p. 10.

[7] V. T. Armstrong, "The Far Eastern Division," *Review and Herald* (June 13, 1946), pp. 155-157; W. P. Bradley and V. T. Armstrong, "An Evening with the Far Eastern Division," *Review and Herald* (June 20, 1946), pp. 227-229.

[8] (General Conference Reports). Nine German families were interned in May, 1940, for six years. Altogether eighty-seven men, women, and children were in concentration camps during the war. Seven of them died.

[9] *Time*. (December 24, 1945).

[10] *Pacific Union Recorder* (October 17, 1945), p. 8.

[11] For the *Far Eastern Division* statistics looked good in 1945:186 new appointees and 99 returning missionaries. These 285 people, however, would face very traumatic conditions. See E. D. Dick, "Forth to the Ripening Harvest Fields: Missionary Sailings in 1945" *Review and Herald* (March 7, 1946), p. 1.

[12] *Review and Herald* (January 30, 1947), p. 17. Of five ships sailing westward from the U.S. one carried 900 passengers. Seven hundred of them were missionaries.

16. Reconstruction in the Philippines

In late 1946 Andrew Nelson was discharged from his responsibilities on General MacArthur's staff. With his assignment in the reconstruction of the Japan ended, he could return to church employment. He was called to the presidency of Philippine Union College in Caloocan City, a suburb of Manila.

There he would restructure the war-torn campus. Also, in a special way, he would restructure some very desperate lives. Andrew and Vera Nelson arrived in Manila in January 1947.[1]

The destruction of the city shocked them. The Philippine Islands had been mauled mercilessly for six years, and the inventory of damages was appalling. Losses included 116 churches, four mission offices, three academies and ten foreign missionary homes. On the city compound in Pasay the Union office had been destroyed. As for the Manila Sanitarium, the departing Japanese troops had totally gutted the building.[2]

The college campus had been headquarters for the occupying Japanese forces for at least five years, and it needed extensive restoration. It also required the benefit of Nelson's unique concept of what an Adventist college should look like. Although the college buildings had been spared, everything else from the library books to industrial equipment had been looted. With a large appropriation from the General Conference and with the eager cooperation of the Filipino teachers, however, rehabilitation went forward at a pace that even Andrew Nelson could approve. He wrote enthusiastically of his strong faculty with their "high spirituality" and "scholastic attainments."

Although English was the language of the educated, thousands of people in Manila understood only the dialects. The foreign missionaries, of course, were encouraged to learn the local speech. As people who had spoken Japanese for many years, however, the Nelsons found Tagalog no great challenge. As for Andrew's fluency in the Japanese language, it would not be wasted. He would use it in a way that neither he nor anyone else could have predicted when he arrived in Manila.

Memories of the pine forests and mountains of Japan, at times, made the heat of Manila seem almost "unbearable." Still the abundance of "bananas, papaya, and mangoes" gave Vera some consolation. When they picked a twenty-seven-pound jackfruit in their own back yard, Andrew recorded the event. "And," he added, "we like the Filipino people so very much." The Nelsons rejoiced in the little daily improvements that indicated that life on campus would get back to normal, eventually.

In the new administration of Philippine Union College Dr. Reuben Manalaysay served as the Vice-President. His was a war story of unrelenting abuse. While Andrew Nelson had been coping with the Thought Police in Japan, Dr. "Man" fell prey to the same evil in Manila. He served as Acting President of PUC during the Japanese occupation of the Philippines. Recipient of a Fulbright Scholarship, he had had one year of study leave in the United States. He was also a celebrated violin soloist and concert performer.

He suffered profoundly because of his contact with Americans. Accusing him of being a spy, the Japanese declared him to be one who had helped the Americans in the defense of the Bataan Peninsula. "You have plans in your head," they snarled. "If you don't tell us, we will crack open your head to see them." Tortured, beaten, and hung upside down for hours, Manalaysay somehow survived. And he did so without bitterness. "My hands and arms were paralyzed for a long time. That experience really taught me how to pray."

Even the Adventist workers in the rural Philippines who had escaped imprisonment still lived on the margins of survival. They were suspected by both Japanese and Filipino soldiers. Speaking of the total lack of transportation, Pastor Gil de Guzman told of his "happy pleasure to hike nearly 2,000 miles" through knee-deep mud visiting churches during the war years.

Under Nelson's leadership Philippine Union College began to flourish. His first year brought in 137 students. By the sixth year enrollment jumped to 800. All of the young people, he guaranteed, were getting the "three-fold head, hand, and heart" education.

Especially he loved his class in Principles of Christian Education. He experimented with the forty-five students by using the

"Morrison System of Master Teaching." He was thrilled "to be able to teach without grades, without final examinations. . . .Without so much of that artificial motivation, I find that there is a much pleasanter relationship between my students and me than when I used the old system of grades." (For the sake of the records "M" stood for "mastery" and would transfer into a "B." MI was "mastery with special interest," and that would be translated as "A").

One vexing, long-standing problem remained. People outside of the college compound imposed their "looseness, immorality, and wickedness" on the campus. Thefts occurred daily, and shootings (involving deaths) were painfully common. The police seemed to be "in cahoots" with the gangs and bandits. When crimes were committed, everyone seemed to know who had done it. Bringing these thugs to justice, however, appeared to be virtually impossible.

Not surprisingly, it was on Nelson's watch at Philippine Union College that the idea of moving the college out of the city evolved into a concrete plan. As he had with Japan Missionary College many years earlier, Nelson had a checklist of requirements for the new property. In July of 1959, an attractive place had been found in Lucban. Unfortunately, delay in the higher levels of administration and fears concerning the squatters who were strongly disinclined to leave the land caused the whole plan to fall through. "We could have managed the squatters," Nelson muttered under his breath.

Many years passed, but the vision was never wholly lost. At last, in 1972, a new home for PUC was purchased on a mountainside at Puting Kahoy, Silang, in the province of Cavite. The missionary spirit of the pioneers enabled administrators, faculty, and students to leave behind the conveniences of city life and to sacrifice, time, energy and effort to make the move. Finally, on August 1, 1996, PUC was granted University status and became Adventist University of the Philippines.

Andrew Nelson would have been so proud of that move, when it finally materialized. Back in post-war Manila, however, he was disappointed. Nonetheless, there remained one more college for him to establish. One more place for him to fulfill his powerful vision for Christian education.

Meanwhile, Andrew became involved in a unique part of the "Reconstruction in the Philippines." It was almost as if he'd been preparing for the job for the last twenty-five years. After the Japanese surrender in Tokyo General MacArthur set up a War Crimes Board to investigate military atrocities. Although a few Americans were court-martialed for heavy-handed treatment of the Filipinos, the subsequent War Trials concerned Japanese prisoners-of-war and were left up to the local courts.

As the Philippine Court handed down death sentences,[3] cases of corruption began to surface. Charges were being made about false witnesses. The prosecution showed photographs of the accused and made the witnesses memorize their faces. Then at trial they could "identify" the prisoners and testify against them. As these things came to his attention, Nelson heatedly declared: "It is not safe to trust implicitly the testimony of a foreigner who claims to be able to identify a Japanese."

In spite of known injustices,[4] post-war Asia literally floated on a sea of emotion. Everyone was in a hurry to see justice done. The Japanese prisoners were often tried in batches, pronounced guilty, and then hustled off to execution. Especially vulnerable were the officers who had been commandants of the prisoner-of-war camps. The courts did not always go by strict rules of evidence or by careful laws of procedure. Truly, the Filipinos, above all, had much to forgive for the long years of Japanese occupation and oppression.

Andrew Nelson, on the other hand, was uniquely qualified to see *both* sides of the post-war fall-out in Asia. Few others could better understand the mindset of the imprisoned Japanese officers facing trials in Manila.

The worst humiliation a Japanese soldier could suffer was, first, to be captured by the enemy. Second, given his defeat, to be executed on the gallows. With full knowledge, both American and Filipino lawyers and judges knew that hanging was the final insult. The proud "sword culture" of the *samurai*—the *bushido*-- has never completely disappeared, even today. For that very reason the Philippine courts made the gallows the standard mode of execution for the prisoners.

To begin with, two dramatic trials captured the world stage. First, an American tribunal hastily sentenced the notorious Tomoyuki Yamashita (1885-1948)[5] to death by hanging. Questions about the unprofessional conduct of the prosecuting officers circulated, and the case even went to the Supreme Court. In the end, there was no reprieve. Yamashita's trial ran parallel to those of a large number of Japanese officers in New Bilibid Prison, near Manila. Some of the lapses that surrounded his trial also marked theirs.

On February 23, 1946, Yamashita climbed the thirteen steps to the gallows at Los Banos Prison Camp south of Manila. Just a year earlier many hundreds of prisoners–of-war (including several Seventh-day Adventist families) had been delivered from the camp by a dramatic parachute drop.[6] Observers considered this the proper place for Yamashita to die. With impeccable Japanese politeness, Yamashita paid respect to his enemies and thanked the Manila court for its "kindful attitude." He also thanked each of his captors, praying that "the gods [would] bless them."

Then came General Hideki Tojo (1884-1948), considered the "poster child" for all Japanese war prisoners. As the Pacific War began to wind down in 1944, he knew that Japan could not win. In good *samurai* form he resigned his offices and planned suicide. Among the first forty alleged war criminals, he was arrested in his home in Setagaya on September 8, 1945. As the American military police burst in, they found that a doctor had carefully marked the position of Tojo's heart on his chest. Clumsily, he'd shot himself but had hit his stomach instead. "I am sorry it is taking me so long to die," he murmured.

Blood gushing from his wound, he was taken to a U.S. Army Hospital where he recovered from his injuries. In due course, a U. S. Army dentist made a new set of upper dentures for Tojo. As a bonus service, he incised the phrase "Remember Pearl Harbor" on them. "I wanted him to live with those words in his mouth at all times," the dentist explained. "I thought that would be good for him."

Somehow the story leaked out, and the dentist's superior officer ordered him to erase the inscription. On the pretext of "cleaning" the dentures, the doctor ordered Tojo back to his office and obeyed orders.

Three years later, in Yokohama, Tojo stood trial for war crimes[7] and received an "A-class" death sentence. In GI salvage clothes, he (at age sixty-five), along with seven other prime prisoners, shuffled off to the gallows on December 25, 1948.[8] These toothless old men represented the ultimate defeat and humiliation of Tojo's plan for a Japanese empire.

Between November 6, 1947 and February 19, 1949 the Philippine courts handed down death sentences to a large number of Japanese prisoners-of-war. In the midst of these trials, however, something remarkable was about to occur at New Bilibid Prison, Muntinglupa. The Seventh-day Adventist Army Chaplain William Bergherm invited Andrew Nelson to preach to the prisoners.

Nelson and his team of Philippine Union College faculty members were joined by Eugene A. Hessel, pastor of the Ellinwood Church. Thus, a weekly prison ministry began. They created a near-perfect kind of ministry. Hessel had been working for Bilibid prisoners for many years. Nelson's fluency in the Japanese language enabled them to converse intimately with the POWs and to understand their situation fully.

Given the circumstances, one might scorn the "jailhouse conversions" brought about by Nelson's ministry to the Japanese officers facing death. On the other hand, who could protest when Dr. Manalaysay himself joined the Bilibid team. Among the 250 prisoners he actually found the man who had tortured him. That man became a Christian,[9] and that was only one of many stories that went round the world.

Concurrently with his daily work, Andrew had family concerns at home. He had, for example, always watched out for his little sister Vivian especially when her divorce left her with two children, Mitzi and Billy, to parent alone.[10]

Vivian gave a lifetime to teaching. In fact, back in 1931 when she'd married Elwyn Smith, she taught school while he went to college. She took care not to tell anyone that she had a husband, because married women usually were not hired to teach. They were expected to stay "in their place." Moreover, if they did find a job they often were not considered worthy of a salary. Or, at least, only a very small one. After all, they had husbands to support them, didn't they?

On one occasion while Andrew was visiting family in Southern California, he offered to look over Vivian's budget to see what he could suggest to help her stretch her paycheck. She and the children were excited. They'd have Andrew all to themselves for the evening! They were sure he'd be a big help.

Andrew and Vivian sat beside each other on the couch, reviewing each category of her budget. Suddenly, he asked, "How much do you want to set aside for new books each month?" Absolutely all of the money had already been allotted. Andrew turned to his sister in alarm. "How. . .how. . .will you buy books?"

"Well," Vivian sighed, "I guess we just won't be buying any books."

"No books?" Andrew threw up his hands and shut his notebook. Not being able to buy books was an emergency totally beyond his comprehension. He simply gave up trying to organize his little sister.

Fortunately, Lynwood Academy had an excellent library, and the family were able to borrow books there. Thus they could still pursue the innate Nelson compulsion for learning.

Years earlier, from her home at 1208 Shelby Street in Seattle, Mama Gustava Nelson had watched her children succeed. She never forgot how much she wanted to be a teacher. "But now," she would proudly remark, "I have five teachers in my family!"[11]

This vitality went far beyond any classrooms. Her eldest daughter Gertrude taught school in Southern California until her husband George Bergman finished medical school (Loma Linda CME, Class of 1924). Then they went to work in Ethiopia.[12]

Andrew, of course, had long ago set out on his academic path. Both of his brothers became physicians. Reuben (Loma Linda CME, Class of 1936) and Philip (Loma Linda CME, Class of 1936) went into partnership together and set up the first medical clinic outside of downtown Seattle in about 1940.[13] Papa Nelson built a beautiful office building for them there.

The first break in the Nelson family circle came suddenly. Mama Gustava entered Portland Sanitarium for surgery. Complications followed, and she died on December 19, 1931. Andrew and Vera were on the other side of the world in Japan when the telegram arrived. As has so often been the case, they could not go home to share in the sorrow of their family.

Papa Andrew lived on alone for another eleven years at 1208 Shelby Street. Then he moved to Southern California where he helped Vivian buy a house in Downey. She was teaching English at Lynwood Academy,[14] and he lived with her for the last four years of his life.

So Anders/Andrew Nelson died on April 8, 1948, just before his eighty-third birthday. He went with no regrets, full of days and beloved of his family. The results of his long-ago leap of faith had spread around the world. Once again, his first son Andrew stationed in the Philippines could not come home to say good-bye.

[1] The Andrew Nelsons sailed from San Francisco aboard the *SS Marine Lynx* on December 15, 1946. "Recent Missionary Departures," *Review and Herald* (January 9, 1947), p. 13.

[2] M. E. Loewen, "Progress in the Philippine Union." *Australasian Record* (August 25, 1947), p. 8. During their time of occupation, the Japanese had taken over both

the Manila and the Penang hospitals. See V. T. Armstrong, "An Evening with the Far Eastern Division," *Review and Herald* (June 20, 1946), pp. 227.

[3] They described three "degrees of innocence.," basing their conclusions on their own observations and a list compiled by Mr. Matsuzaki: (See Appendix III, p. 138.) "Japanese Prisoners Wrongfully Sentenced to Death by Hanging." The cases of some of the victimized Japanese officers even came to the attention of the U. S. Supreme Court.

[4] Numerous "makeshift trials" occurred in the Philippines, China, Southeast Asia and Indonesia.

[5] Yamashita is known as "The Tiger of Malaya" for his success in defeating Malaya and Singapore. He arrived to take charge of the Japanese forces in the Philippines just days before U. S. troops landed in Leyte to recapture the islands.

[6] On February 23, 1945, U. S. troops had dropped behind enemy lines to rescue 2100 prisoners from the Los Banos Concentration Camp. On the same day, after losing 8,000 soldiers, the U. S. flag was raised over Iwo Jima. The latter event captured media attention much more readily than the Los Banos Raid.

[7] Tojo was found guilty on seven counts: (1) Wars of aggression, (27) Unprovoked war against China, (29) Unprovoked war against the United States (Pearl Harbor, (31, 32, 33) Unprovoked wars against the British Commonwealth, the Netherlands/ Indonesia, and France/Indo-china, and (54) Inhumane treatment of Prisoners-of-War. Tojo was also considered directly responsible for the murders of four million Chinese. http://en.wikipedia.org/wiki/Hideki_Tojo. (October 2010).

[8] Gavin Davis, *Prisoners of the Japanese: POW's of World War II in the Pacific* (New York: William Morrow, Inc., 1994), pp. 368-371. The Japanese despised whoever surrendered. By the Bushido Code, suicide was the norm. Until recent times, the head of a failed company or a student who failed his examinations was expected to commit suicide. Today, resignation—sometimes—is sufficient.

[9] *North Pacific Union Gleaner* (September 24, 1951), p. 1.

[10] Vivian and Elwyn Smith divorced in 1945 after he came home from service in World War II. A pilot, he flew cargo planes over the Burma Hump into China. He earned two Distinguished Flying Crosses.

[11] The Nelson children all taught school in various places at various times: Andrew: Oriens in Seattle, followed by decades in Japan, the Philippines, and finally at La Sierra College. Gertrude: Seattle, Bremerton, and Ethiopia. Philip: Gem State Academy and Lodi Academy. Reuben: Mount Ellis Academy. Vivian: Seattle, Hong Kong, Santa Monica, Lynwood Academy, La Sierra College.

[12] Dr. and Mrs. Bergman served in Ethiopia and established the first Seventh-day Adventist hospital in Dessie. George sent his family to Cairo to avoid the Italian invasion, but they returned too soon and were involved in the upheaval anyway. After returning to the U. S. in 1938, George went into private practice. Later, he was drafted into the army and was stationed in Bolivia for the duration of World War II. Ultimately, the Bergmans set up practice in Montebello, California.

[13] During World War II, Philip (in Family Practice) kept the Seattle practice running while Reuben served in the Army at the Fitzsimmons Hospital in Denver. After the war, Reuben did his residency in OB/GYN.

[14] After teaching at Lynwood Academy for eighteen years, Vivian became Dean of Women at La Sierra College, retiring in 1976. She married Lester Cushman, Professor of Physics, Mathematics and Astronomy at La Sierra. She researched Nelson genealogy and made several trips to Sweden, finally producing *Stories from the Family of 1208* in 2006 (114 pages).

17. A Unique Prison Ministry

Over a period of two years Andrew Nelson and his chaplaincy team conducted a complete series of Bible studies in New Bilibid Prison in Muntinglupa, near Manila.

When nineteen Japanese officers were ready for baptism, Nelson persuaded the War Trials officials to allow the baptism to be held on the campus of Philippine Union College. The military police vehicles surged out into the chaotic Manila traffic, following Nelson's little black Chrysler all of the way out to Caloocan City. After a blessed Sabbath morning together, hundreds of people watched the quiet campus service as former enemies became brothers in the faith.

The Japanese prisoners of war in Bilibid were neither the first nor the last to suffer injustice and to be executed as innocent men. Andrew Nelson and his fellow chaplain, Eugene A. Hessel (Pastor of the Ellinwood Church) went to great lengths to save those officers in Bilibid who were manifestly innocent but condemned to the gallows nonetheless. The two pastors determined to discover the real circumstances of each crime that came up in the trials

Unfortunately, the identification of the Japanese soldiers could be very haphazard. Caucasians have a great variety of distinguishing marks: Red or blonde hair, freckles, blue or green eyes, curly or straight hair, and so forth. Many foreigners looking at Asians, blacks, and Latinos can find fewer differentiating characteristics. What can be said beyond black hair, brown eyes and dark(er) skin? Everyone looks alike.

In the heat of revenge that prevailed after World War II, few people cared to examine the cases of mistaken identity. As Nelson pointed out, it became altogether too "easy for one Japanese to be mistaken for another." Some of the vindictive, war-weary people in Manila simply decided that "as long as they are Japs we might as well hang one as the other. At least, we get revenge."

Andrew Nelson and Eugene Hessel worked diligently, however, to save the lives of a number of prisoners they deemed innocent.[1] They studied case after case in minute detail.

One day, in the course of conversation with the POWs at Bilibid, the subject of innocents being condemned to the gallows along with the guilty came up. One of the prisoners, Hideichi Matsuzaki, spoke up, "I know who's innocent and who's guilty."

At first a very "tough customer," his attending the Adventist meetings had mellowed him considerably. In fact, Matsuzaki was "developing into a fine Christian gentleman." He was personally fortunate in that because he had been credited with rescuing President Quirino out of Fort Santiago, his own sentence had been commuted to twenty years.

After interviewing his fellow prisoners, Matuzaki Hideichi, made a careful survey[2] and singled out the ones whose sentences he considered unjust. "I have no sympathy," he declared, "for the vicious and renegade Japanese who perpetrated unspeakable atrocities that shocked the world." Moreover, he did not include the names of men whom he did not know well. He tidily classified the prisoners at three levels of guilt:

1. Those with absolutely no connection with the crime,
2. Those who might have been at the scene of the crime but were not responsible parties,
3. Those who might have had something to do with the crime (or one phase of it), but for whom the death penalty is "far too severe."

Next, Andrew Nelson immersed himself in case after case among the condemned Japanese officers. He spent hours in counseling, interviews, correspondence with the prisoners and their families in Japan, appeals to the Philippine court, and requests to church administrators. He spared no effort on behalf of "his men" in Bilibid prison. (See "Prisoner Lists," Appendix III, p. 138)

One stricken family in Tokyo, for instance, watched in horror as their only son, **Kose Yasumasa**, was sentenced to the gallows.[3] They argued that the massacre at Lual had been carried out by the 4th Company, 2nd Battalion, as the Admiral testified. Kose commanded a different unit. Also, the medical officer certified that the day of the killings, Kose was delirious with fever and could not have been present. Like so many others this appeal failed.

Dr. **Minotaro Tatokoro** became known as the "Cannibal Killer."[4] Rising to almost 9,511 feet Kitanglad is a long-dormant volcano in Bukidnon, Mindanao. At the beginning of the Japanese occupation, the troops in this beautiful area had success. Then, with the return of General MacArthur, guerrilla activities increased. The Japanese found foraging for food both difficult and dangerous, and the remnants of the Imperial Army were literally starving.

One day Corporal Tatokoro's superior officer approached him. "Take one of the Filipino prisoners and kill him. We need to eat. Besides, you're a doctor, so you'll know how to do the butchering most expertly." A committed Shintoist, Tatokoro obeyed the gruesome order, and the soldiers ate for one more day.

When he finally arrived in Bilibid and the war trials began, Tatokoro knew that his case was hopeless. Actually, to save some of his fellow prisoners, he even confessed to crimes he hadn't committed. His rich, new Christian experience enabled him to lose all interest in militaristic Shinto as well as in works-driven Buddhism. He became superintendent of the Bilibid Sabbath School and loved singing gospel songs in the prison sextet.

"His life will be worth more than his death, considering the rising threat of Communism," Tatokoro's friends argued. Still, nothing of his new Christian love and faith could eradicate his past. Before his execution, however, he rejoiced to know that his family was attending Christian meetings in Kujikawa, near his home.

Then there was the unusual case of Lieutenant **Katsuyoshi Taninaka** who commanded a thirty-man garrison of Japanese troops in Calbayog in Samar. His good works earned him the title of the "Father of Calbayog." On July 16, 1948, a large legal document was presented to the War Trials Commission to modify Taninaka's sentence to the gallows. The fifteen resolutions revealed a surprising personality, and his virtues far outstripped those of the vicious local police constable who hated him and the villagers.

He established a food distribution system, the "Foodstuff Association." He secured relief funds and used his own money to educate the children of the town. With uncanny foresight he observed: "After all, the Japanese may not win this war."

So Taninaka preserved the American textbooks that were supposed to have been destroyed. He took medical supplies from his garrison's own stores to treat hundreds of people with malaria, beriberi, and skin diseases. He made provisions for abandoned old people and for maternity care. He treated everyone alike, regardless of race. When his men rounded up Filipino guerrillas, Taninaka the Shintoist required them to attend church and make "confession to the bishop." Taninaka's wife Sugio wrote to Dr. Nelson. He tried to save her husband's life, but to no avail.

With the help of Matuzaki's insightful list, Nelson and others actively engaged in appeals to the Philippine Court, and their work made news. On the front page of the Manila *Evening News* on September 3, 1949, for instance, a flamboyant article reported the efforts of the chaplains who had served the prisoners in New Bilibid Prison. "Missionaries Bat for Japs, Some Doomed Nips 'Innocent' Claim."

Letters, sworn statements, and appeals from this period of Andrew's life testify to the wholehearted efforts he put forth to see justice done. At one point, he approached President Quirino himself. While diplomatically congratulating him for his efforts to foster "a democratic spirit" amid the chaos of post-war Philippines, he vouched for the sincerity of the doomed Japanese prisoners whom he had "baptized into Christianity."

The Philippines, Nelson argued, had long been a Christian country. If some of the prisoners' lives could be preserved, they would be "living witnesses to the efficacy of Christianity and the power of the gospel to save even the vilest of criminals." Commuting their death sentences could "establish friendly relations between the Filipino and Japanese people" and promote peace. Indeed, such a measure would be a high-water mark of Quirino's administration and exhibit the magnanimous Christian spirit that could set the Philippines apart from all of its Asian neighbors.[5]

On another occasion Nelson and Hessel sent a carefully prepared two-page letter to Judge Esguerra,[6] urging him to "do something to prevent the punishment of the innocent" and to see that "justice prevails." The two pastors recoiled from the possibility of being called to "minister at the gruesome ceremony of the hanging of the innocents." They offered, once again, Matsuzaki's insightful document because they considered it to " be a truer picture than one might think of the guilt or innocence of the men [he listed]." A report as "sincere, honest, and invaluable picture of innocence" as would be possible to find, they said.[7]

By and large, however, the appeals went unheard. Teodoro Evangelista, Executive Secretary to President Quirino, notified

Andrew Nelson of the executive decision. The Philippines had simply suffered too much. (He referred to the finality of the Nurenberg trials in Germany.) The Philippines, "as a small nation," must take care of her security needs. Therefore, the President has decided that he cannot "grant a blanket commutation" of the death sentences.[8] Subsequently Andrew attend the execution of fourteen of the prisoners in Bilibid.

Two weeks after the liberation of the prisoners in Los Banos in 1945, the Japanese authorities had massacred 1500 villagers as a reprisal. This event, accounted, in part, for the severity of the court decisions at Bilibid four years later. There were, however, a few survivors. Some prisoners made it back to Japan to finish their prison sentences at home. Eventually they were released in their homeland.

One of them was Dr. **Haruo Ichinose**. In 1943 he had graduated at the top of his class in the Medical Faculty at Tokyo Imperial University. He became a surgeon in one of the naval units of Rear Admiral Takesue Furuse stationed in Infanta, Quezon, where a massacre occurred. Along with thirteen other officers Ichinose was sentenced to hang.[9] Already a Christian, he joined Nelson's group in Bilibid and became a very articulate spokesman for the new Seventh-day Adventists there. Support poured in. How could "such a mild tempered and spiritually minded person" be guilty of brutality? Indeed, he cared for sick fellow-prisoners without regard for his own health. A fine physician, he ultimately served on the medical staff of Tokyo Adventist Hospital.

Other survivors of Bilibid included the scholarly Major **Isao Ichimura** who eventually joined the faculty of Japan Union College, and **Masataka Kobayashi** who worked as a colporteur.[10]

Years passed, however, and the men scattered. Perhaps many lost their way. Still, memories of those intense days that Andrew Nelson spent chaplaining the New Bilibid Prisoners of War could never destroy his confidence. "I will see many of them in the Kingdom," he affirmed.

"Oyasumi nasai. Ashita mata omeni kakarimasu"
("Goodnight. I'll see you in the morning.") was their watchword.[11]

[1] Andrew Nelson, "The Names of the Japanese Prisoners That I Believe Have Been Condemned in Spite of Their Being Innocent." Philippine Union College, nd.

[2] Matazuki's own death sentence had been reduced to twenty years. See Appendix II, "Japanese Prisoners Wrongfully sentenced to Death by Hanging." p. 137.

[3] Letter to President Elpidio Quirino, from Taihachi Kose (father), Chiyogiku Kose (mother), and Hiroko Kose (wife). Kose had never seen his seven-year-old son. Tokyo, April 15, 1951.

[4] A. N. Nelson, "Minotaro Tatokoro's Experience." Unpublished manuscript. nd.

[5] Letter: A. N. Nelson, President, Philippine Union College of Seventh-day Adventists, to Elpidio Quirino, President of the Philippine Republic, Malacanang Palace, Manila, nd. Co-signers: Thomas A. Pilar (Department of Theology, PUC); A. Z. Roda (President, Northern Luzon Mission); N. S. Mallari (Librarian, PUC); A. M. Adams (President, Philippine Union Mission of SDA); N. A. Munson (Manager, Manila Sanitarium and Hospital).

[6] Letter, from Andrew Nelson and Eugene Hessel, to Judge Esguerra, May 27, 1949.

[7] Andrew Nelson, Tr. "The Names of the Japanese Prisoners That I believe Have Been condemned In Spite of Their Being Innocent." Philippine Union College, nd. Letter, to Judge Esguerra, from A. N. Nelson and Eugene Hessel, May 27, 1949.

[8] Letter from Teodoro Evangelista to Domingo C. Bascara, YMCA, Manila (January 10, 1951).

[9] Haruo Ichinose was baptized on October 25, 1949. In 1951 Nelson appealed his case twice, April 24 and July 30. See www.adventistarchives.org. (June 2010)

[10] W. P. Bradley, "Converted Japanese War Prisoners Now in Church Work" *Australasian Record* (April 11, 1955), p. 7.

[11] Letter from Andrew Nelson to E. M. Adams, April 14, 1965.

The Japan Years

1. The only hatless one in the group, Andrew Nelson headed up the survey team preparing for the building of Japan Missionary College in Chiba Ken, Naraha (about 1925). He wrote exuberantly that "spring has just broken upon us, and students and teachers are busy in the woods, and fields, and shops."

2. Construction of the buildings on the new Naraha campus was an intense, do-it-ourselves project.

3. No one could resist the charm of the tame deer that sometimes emerged from the cool forests of Japan.

4. Vera Nelson's garden at the college was the best on campus indisputably. Here she harvested new green peas. Her gardens also maintained a blaze of flowers every season.

外人住宅

5. An unknown Japanese artist has interpreted the early structures on the campus of Japan Missionary College at Naraha, Chiba Ken, erected by students and staff. Above: The three missionary faculty homes. The Andrew Nelson family lived in the middle one for a dozen years.
6. Below: A partial view of the Administration Building. (Courtesy of Dr. Louis Venden.)

チャペル玄関

7. The fifteen children at Amanuma (Tokyo Hospital Compound), Japan, in the 1920's. Their body language and facial expressions indicate that most of them would have preferred not to pose in this line-up.
From R-L, tallest to shortest: 1) Albert Cole, 2) Charles Anderson, 3) Marie Armstrong, 4) Ruth Cole, 5) Victor Armstrong, 6) Richard Nelson, 7) Virginia Anderson (Hilliard), 8) Alfred Webster, 9) Esther Cole, 10) Evelyn Kraft (Wallace), 11) Beth Armstrong, 12-13, twins) Dorothy Nelson (Oster) and Donald Nelson, 14) Harry Webster, 15) Lotus Perkins. (Photo courtesy of Louis Venden)

8. The twins, Dorothy and Donald, played with their kittens, Blacky and Booty, in their garden at Naraha. They never forgot the week the family went on vacation, leaving the neighbor, Mrs. Millard in charge of the cats. Blacky refused to eat until he brought his brother Booty in to share the food with him.

9. In the Great Tokyo Earthquake of 1923 the Signs Press building collapsed.

10. The Nelson home at Naraha held a lifetime of happy memories for the whole family.

11. Far Eastern Academy was founded to provide high school-level education for the children of expatriate missionaries. When it opened in Shanghai, China (1926), it was housed in this building  that represented the best architectural form of the day (Now the government Department of Education). At the end of World War II, FEA re-opened in Singapore and remained there until it closed in 1992.

12. When the Nelsons received a 1929 Model A Ford as a gift from their old friend Joe Hall, it proved to be an enormous asset. Out of the car, Vera enjoys the ocean scenery on the road to Kobe, Japan.

13. Lake Nojiri was a favorite vacation destination for foreign residents in central Japan. Father Andrew and (later) son Richard Nelson owned two little adjoining cabins on the wooded hillside, with a beautiful view of the lake. These were  part of a seven-house community owned by the Seventh-day Adventist missionaries.

14. Being at Nojiri was fine any season of the year. While the others enjoyed skiing, however, Andrew Nelson would often put in sixteen-hour days working on his Japanese-English dictionary.

15. The second furlough in 1933 involved many thousands of travel miles. Here they negotiated the Panama Canal aboard the Katsu Agrimaru.

16.

16. Once in New York, the Nelsons took delivery of a 1933 Chevrolet for the long drive across the continent, back home to Seattle.

17. 1933 Portrait of Vera and Andrew Nelson.

17.

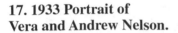

18.

18. Harassed by the urgency of super-jet travel, we can scarcely remember the days of the ocean liners. Aboard the Rotterdam, Andrew and Vera Nelson learned how to relax and simply enjoy the Pacific crossing. What if it did take a month?

World War II

旅客以外の方は入れません

DEPARTING PASSENGERS ONLY

19. In 1940, because of the threat of war in the Pacific, the Far Eastern Division Committee ordered all missionaries in Japan to evacuate. With the twins at Far Eastern Academy in Shanghai and Richard at Walla Walla College back home, Andrew and Vera left Tokyo for Shanghai. Their smiles belied the gravity of the situation.

20. Holding the civilian equivalent of the rank of Colonel, Andrew N. Nelson served on General MacArthur's staff. After Japan signed the Instruments of Surrender aboard the Missouri on August 15, 1945, Lt. Richard Nelson went to Tokyo, followed by his father Andrew N. Nelson and Francis Millard a week later. Richard represented the U. S. Strategic Bombing Survey, charged with assessing the effectiveness of the final bombing of Japan.

War Department

Office of the Chief of Staff

Commendation for Meritorious Civilian Service

To Whom It May Concern:

Dr. Andrew N. Nelson

has received official commendation and praise

for outstanding performance of duty.

Citation:

For initiative in undertaking lexicographical projects
designed to effect great saving of time for government
agencies, for his brilliant sense of organization and
unflagging devotion to duty and for his readiness to
forget self in order to put his talents at the service
of others.

26 February 1946.

Thos T Handy
Deputy Chief of Staff

21. This certificate from the U. S. War Department commended Andrew for four years of "civilian military" service. (Awarded on February 26, 1946)

The Philippines

22. In its infancy, the farm at Mountain View College, Bukidnon, Philippines (1956).

23. One of MVC's first industries was a little sugar mill (1956).

24. Todd Murdoch was the president who first was able to carry out Andrew Nelson's ardent work-study vision that became the foundation of Mountain View College. Nelson's interest in the project never failed, and he considered the Scots-Canadian the ideal man for the job.

25. This aerial view of Mountain View College Campus shows the well ordered layout that Andrew Nelson envisioned from the start of this ambitious venture in education.

26. On October 29, 1949, Andrew Nelson baptized Major Isao Ichimura, along with eighteen other Japanese prisoners-of-war on the campus of Philippine Union College. Pardoned at the end of the war, Ichimura became head of the Japanese Language Department at Japan Missionary College. (Photo by C. Brion)

27. Years later, Andrew Nelson was celebrated on the "This is Your Life" program in Tokyo. One of his prisoner friends, 400 miles away, captured this picture off of his television screen.

28. Retirement years gave Andrew Nelson time to devote to his dictionary writing.

29. First published in 1962, Nelson's Modern Reader's Japanese-English Character Dictionary **was hailed as "the first really practical, completely up-to-date, and authoritative dictionary in its field in almost 50 years." It continues to be a genuinely important book to all English-speaking students of written Japanese.**

30. This is one of the latest revised versions of Andrew Nelson's Japanese-English Character Dictionary. **They are still based on Andrew's Classic Edition.**

1. Sample pages from Nelson's Japanese dictionary show how efficiently he helped the student find the characters and then identify their most current readings. The dictionary was later revised by the Japanese Language Department of the University of Hawaii.

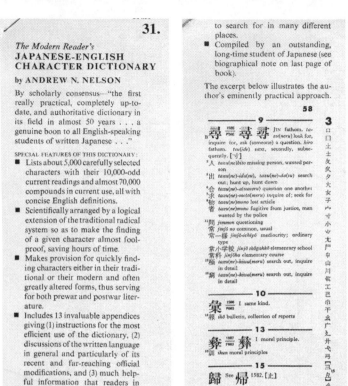

31.

The Modern Reader's
JAPANESE-ENGLISH CHARACTER DICTIONARY
by ANDREW N. NELSON

By scholarly consensus—"the first really practical, completely up-to-date, and authoritative dictionary in its field in almost 50 years . . . a genuine boon to all English-speaking students of written Japanese . . ."

SPECIAL FEATURES OF THIS DICTIONARY:

- Lists about 5,000 carefully selected characters with their 10,000-odd current readings and almost 70,000 compounds in current use, all with concise English definitions.

- Scientifically arranged by a logical extension of the traditional radical system so as to make the finding of a given character almost fool-proof, saving hours of time.

- Makes provision for quickly finding characters either in their traditional or their modern and often greatly altered forms, thus serving for both prewar and postwar literature.

- Includes 13 invaluable appendices giving (1) instructions for the most efficient use of the dictionary, (2) discussions of the written language in general and particularly of its recent and far-reaching official modifications, and (3) much helpful information that readers in Oriental fields have heretofore had

(continued on back flap)

to search for in many different places.
- Compiled by an outstanding, long-time student of Japanese (see biographical note on last page of book).

The excerpt below illustrates the author's eminently practical approach.

32.

NEW APPROACH

From Oregon to California and from New Guinea to Okinawa, Jacob R. Mittleider has demonstrated that the poorest of soils can produce abundantly — even surpluses — for those who work the land with scientific but simple methods. The hallmark of the Mittleider Method is maximum production. The plan features regular soil testing and balancing the soil with nutrients, early starting of plants in greenhouses to ensure uniform growth in a disease- and insect-free environment until they are strong, careful landscaping, weed-free cultivation, and overall cleanliness.

Orderliness of Mittleider fields is enhanced by the nearly 100 percent survivability of plants.

In **Food For Everyone**, Mittleider and Dr. Andrew N. Nelson, the authors, have captured the vision of a world without hunger — of lands transformed into gardens and of people transformed by hope.

32. Together Andrew N. Nelson and Jacob R. Mittleider wrote the somewhat controversial book Food for Everyone.

33. An extended Nelson Family Reunion, in Bakersfield, California, about 1962, produced a fine crop of children.

34. 1968, Andrew and Vera's 50th wedding anniversary called for high celebration in their home at 5126 Peacock Lane in La Sierra, Riverside, California.

35.

35. At the Far Eastern Division offices in Singapore in November 1972 Dr. Charles B. Hirsch (right) conferred the Merit Award on Andrew Nelson. It honored his half-century of Adventist educational leadership. A proud moment for many people, and no one was more surprised than Andrew N. Nelson himself.

36.

36. Andrew and Vera Nelson posed for their last photograph together in Hong Kong in 1975.

37.

37. Also in retirement, Dorothy Nelson-Oster (age 83) sailed off a three-meter diving board in Colfax, California. This was one of her average of 50 dives a day. Her lifelong love of diving began at age four, in Japan. At Takayama Beach she began by diving off of her Dad's shoulders. Wherever she lived, she managed to find a place to dive.

38. A Nelson Family Reunion at Lake Nojiri, Japan.
Front Row (L-R): Jerry Nelson, Shirley Nelson, Jan Nelson, Shari
Nelson, Donna Nelson, Don Oster, Ellowyn Oster, Cy Oster.
Back/Middle Row (L-R): Richard Nelson, Carol Nelson, Carol Rae
Nelson, Vera Nelson, Barbara Nelson, Andrew Nelson, Don Nelson,
Arlene Nelson, Dorothy Oster, Kenneth Oster.

39. Fine Japanese cloisonné (courtesy of Richard and Carol Nelson). This emerald green vase with the flower design embedded subtly in the enamel was presented to Dr. Richard Nelson by the Egyptian Embassy in Tokyo (1961). While attending an international conference of parliamentarians, the Egyptian Minister of Education was hit by a bus on a Tokyo street. After spending a month in Tokyo Sanitarium, he returned to Cairo still enveloped in casts. As attending physician, Richard even found the opportunity to pray with the Moslem leaders for the man's healing. Afterwards, the Minister was instrumental in making it possible for the Adventist church to retain its school in Heliopolis (near Cairo).

40. Generations of his students can recall this keen, kindly image of Andrew N. Nelson. At his desk and among his books, he was dignified, devout, and sympathetic–always ready to explore a new idea.

41. After Vivian Nelson-Smith-Cushman became the Nelson family historian, she made several trips to Sweden. There she gamely mounted on a painted wooden horse.

18. One More Power College

In the middle of his term as president of Philippine Union College in post-war Manila, Andrew Nelson went back to an old idea. That is, his vision of what a Seventh-day Adventist college was supposed to be like. It had been the mighty force that had fueled the founding of Japan Missionary College in rural Naraha back in 1926.

To be sure, the Philippine Union College campus was a lovely little island of peace and order in the big city. Outside of the compound walls, however, seethed an overcrowded metropolis, oftentimes out of control. Inevitably, the ideal of a different kind of college came back to him full force.

Nelson set about soliciting the interest of the PUC faculty, the Union administrators, all the way up to the Far Eastern Division officers in Singapore. His message was clear and single-minded: "We need a new college in the Philippines. We need space for the kind of work-study program that has always been our ideal."[1]

Andrew established a planning group, and they went back to the three church classics: *Education, Counsels to Parents, Teachers and Students*, and *Fundamentals of Christian Education*. He was back on familiar ground, and enthusiasm ran high on all sides. The Prayer Check List the group produced was, with only a few minor modifications, very like the one he had followed back in Japan.

In April 1950 Nelson set out with Wilton O. Baldwin, "our indefatigable Division Secretary." Their explorations ultimately took them to the southernmost island of Mindanao and up on to the high central plateau. One day the men passed a group of people, the Valendez family, resting under a tree. They turned out to be Seventh-day Adventists who insisted that the two men spend the Sabbath with them. The next day they found themselves in a "thriving church of vo hundred members."

Sunday morning their host gave his visitors exciting news. Over the bountiful breakfast provided he explained, "Somehow we were awake in the middle of the night. God made us remember a place where we went during the wartime days."

Nelson and Baldwin, accompanied by their new-found friends, came to Bukidnon, a place that had been a refuge from the invading Japanese armies. What they saw was "a series of plateaus, one above the other, presenting us with many broad, level, fertile fields with scarcely a stone to be found in them." Plenty of room for school buildings and for a potential farm that would produce "bananas, papayas, pineapples, mangoes, avocados, and all types of citrus fruits." Also, they found thick forests of *abaca*, the tree famous for the fiber that makes strong rope.

At 2,000 feet of elevation, this secluded place was forty miles from the seaport of Cagayan. It was also cool and reputedly beyond the reach of typhoons. Andrew looked over the lovely landscape and could almost see, physically, what a college here might become.

Nelson wrote rhapsodically of what he and Baldwin saw: "There are swift, cool, clear, perennial mountain streams, one of which is twenty feet wide and another 120 feet wide. There are also many fine springs on the land, and the rainfall is made to order. It is practically always clear and sunny in the morning. There are almost daily showers beginning in the middle or late afternoon and at times continuing on into the night. The next morning the sun shines brightly again. This idea for farm work in the mornings and class work in the afternoons would work well. The dry season is only a few weeks long. There are eleven waterfalls, one of which is 120 feet high, just perfect for our hydroelectric power! Next to the farmland is a grand hardwood forest [of Philippine mahogany] of over 12,500 acres. . . [The] sixty-foot trees have diameters of three or four feet."

Further investigation showed that this large piece of land had recently been turned back by a wealthy pre-war American cattle rancher and now belonged to the government. There were, of course, the squatters who had to be dealt with. Although they'd never owned a foot of land, these people had farmed there for years and, therefore, had some rights to stay on, if they wished.

Indeed, a rival buyer was courting the squatters at that very moment. His emissaries became discouraged when they encountered "a giant" at the edge of he property. He threatened to roll their two armed jeeps over the cliff if they didn't turn back. On the spot, they gave up their plan to chase the students and teachers off of the land. Mountain View College, however, has never, at any time, had a protecting giant in residence. Therefore, the story has become part of the school's history of providential leadings.

With a little help from the congressman from Bukidnon, the Adventist church prevailed. He promised the squatters that the college to be built would be the best in the country. They were persuaded to cooperate, accepting help to relocate and get their new fields plowed for the spring planting.

Then there had to be an official survey of the land. The National Irrigation Board in Manila assured them of all water rights. Philippine Air Lines even agreed to make the college a flag stop for their regular commercial planes. The National Forestry Bureau granted logging rights on the 12,500 acres of forest. Finally, by the end of 1951, the Far Eastern Division approved the purchase of the land. Thus, Mountain View College was born.

On January 1, 1952, school began. The first administration building was a bamboo hut six feet above ground. It had a grass roof. "Three cots were located upstairs, and the ground below became the cafeteria. Another bamboo house, formerly occupied by one of the squatters, was renovated for the Virgil Bartlett home. It included a kitchen, shower room, bedroom, and an outside toilet."

The water supply was piped in from a spring 200 feet above these temporary "buildings." Actually both hot and cold water came down, because the sun heated the pipes during the day. It took two more years of living in makeshift housing before real homes could be built. Then came the luxuries of electric stoves, refrigerators, washing machines, and water heaters.

It is hard to over-estimate Andrew N. Nelson's personal investment in the founding of Mountain View College. At Christmas in 1950, while enjoying a cool, mountain-vacation in Baguio (Philippines), he reverted to writing poetry. He did this from time to time, though few people knew that he had this emotional outlet.

He produced more than 200 lines of poetry (in an indeterminate form). He entitled the work "Bukidnon: Ten Years Hence." Subtitled "A Day Dream," it featured himself and Baldwin as "two explorers" (on horseback) with "a band of daring brown men." Their view of the campus begins by moonlight, follows through a day of work and study and ends again at night. The descriptions are quaintly reminiscent of 18th–century speech and tastes.

> Rushing sound of falling water
> Greets them from the canyon yonder
> And their hoofsteps hasten thither
> Down the Valley of Maligon
> Through the stately timbered shadows.

Ten years later (April, 1960), Andrew returned to the poem. Joyfully he put a check mark by each line to indicate that the forecast had been abundantly fulfilled. Only one thing was missing. The telescope on Mount Kisalum,[2] now (suitably) called Mount Nelson. In one more decade, however, even that desire would be fulfilled.

> Others spend the evening hours
> Peering into distant star lands
> Riding speeding light beams swiftly
> To celestial meadows gorgeous.
> Pleiades, Orion's gleaming,
> Comets with their tails a-streaming,
> Ringed planets, tunnels jeweled. . . .

So, the wonderful new college campus had been located.

Now it was time for the Nelsons to begin their furlough leave. The Division Committee had decided that the two campuses, though geographically separated, would be bonded administratively. Nelson would be president of both Philippine Union College and Mountain View College. Likewise Bartlett would be manager of both colleges. The arrangement was a little unusual, given the distance between the two institutions. Nonetheless, because the Bukidnon project was so dear to his heart, Andrew was pleased with the arrangement and believed that it could work.

The bombshell hit Andrew and Vera Nelson while they were in London on their homeward-bound journey. It turned out that there was opposition to the first action about the "double leadership" of PUC and MVC. Oddly enough, that original action never got into the official minutes. So, the decision had been completely negated. Even worse, the Nelsons were not returning to the Philippines at all! How could this happen?

Some people work a lifetime in church service without trauma. Many others, at one time or another, literally have the rug pulled out from under their feet. Rational and well grounded as he was, Andrew Nelson never lost his footing—although he might easily have done so. The pain of this event in London effectively ended the joy of their trip toward home.

During this difficult time Andrew, once more, went back to his master plan for living. It enabled him to survive.

Nelson's Life Principles
(Compiled in 1953)

1. Seek out variety.[4]
2. Be sincere in every word and act.
3. Keep cool, never allowing myself to become irritated.
4. Do it now, and leave future time for advancement.
5. Dispatch matters in the shortest time possible.
6. Seek inspiration for the present and future, rather than the past.
7. Forget past things and concentrate on the now.
8. Carry out plans with boldness.
9. Let good enough alone.
10. Never reveal words I have promised to keep confidential.
11. Never allow myself to feel "blue." I'm a fool if I do.

Eventually, Andrew received a comforting letter from M. C. Warren who felt that if he'd been present at the meeting, "the outcome would have been different." He said: "I feel awfully sorry for you. . . . I feel that the college has made an awful mistake. I do not see how they are going to receive a strong financial backing from the General Conference, if they can throw you overboard like that, without even having a good man in mind to take your place."

Many were praying that Andrew would find "strength to rise above this disappointment." Warren continued: "Were it not for your efforts, we would have nothing in Bukidnon today. It is hard to understand why, after working as you have to get this secured and started, you should be removed before the school is organized and operating." Was it possible that God "has a field for you which is even more important than this one?" Nonetheless, his last sentence remained prophetic: "MVC will ever stand as a monument to your efforts."

No question, Andrew always had a vision of what needed to be done. He also had the leadership ability and the drive to make it happen. That spirit was enough, perhaps, to intimidate certain overly cautious people.

A month later, Andrew replied to Warren's letter. "The staggering thunderbolt" that struck in London had, indeed, brought their trip to "an unhappy ending." His "rude dismissal" notwithstanding, he was pleased to discover that the wonderful Bukidnon story would become an "inspiration all over the Adventist world."

Could he have then seen far enough into the future, Andrew would have known that Mountain View College would move on from victory to victory. With a touch of sadness, however, he concluded: "I am sorry that the venomous criticism has made it impossible for me to help you any more. . . . It's hard enough to be a college president without such stabbing in the back." In keeping with his long-established Life Plan, however, Andrew Nelson would "not stoop to either answer such criticism nor retaliate." Once again, he demonstrated that circumstances only reveal what we are. They don't make us what we are.

It's a sorry tale but one which must be faced. Life simply isn't fair! While administrators doing "God's work" pray for guidance, they also have power. Then they feel "entitled" and tend to think that all of their decisions are flawless. Victims fall by the way, and if all the statistics were brought together the body count would be depressingly high.

The future years at Mountain View College evolved into a pioneering saga. Living on that campus was never for the faint hearted.[3] Some, both students and teachers, fell by the wayside. Life was just too hard, and not everyone could endure the isolation and primitive living conditions. Still, through it all, Andrew Nelson's plan for a "Power College" held. It would be many years, however, before he would realize that his dream had been fulfilled, even though he could not be there to participate in the latter part of the story.

While on furlough Andrew was interviewed on a radio program called "Mission to the World." He was asked: "Has it ever occurred to you to want to secure a comfortable position with a lucrative remuneration?" Obviously, he had the credentials to make that a "possible dream."

"No, I have very little interest in concentrating on the amassing of wealth," he replied. "I enjoy living with the people in the mission fields. My experience of working with the Japanese, Chinese, and Filipinos for thirty years . . . has in itself been a tremendous reward."

In the summer of 1953 Andrew Nelson returned alone to become president of the Japan Union Mission. For him, of course, returning to Japan could never be a "bad thing." Vera, however, had remained at home to nurse her mother back to health. (She succeeded, because her mother lived for six more years).

Since their departure on furlough the previous year had taken such a strange turn, the Nelsons had loose ends to tie up in the Philippines. On the way to the year-end meetings in Singapore, Andrew left early to meet Vera in Manila where they packed up their household goods to ship back to Japan.

The Nelsons had to marvel at how scattered their family had become. Dorothy and her husband Ken (Oster) worked in Persia. Donald and Arlene had a practice in California. To top it all Richard and Carol had just arrived in Tokyo!

Although Richard had known conversational Japanese from childhood, he needed a good tutor now to prepare him for the medical board examinations. He had to pass the written examination (*kanji*) as well as an oral test. Fortunately, he had excellent assistance from the well-educated Major Isao Ichimura. He was one of the prisoners of war at Bilibid who had become a Seventh-day Adventist and had escaped the death sentence to come home. When Richard Nelson went to take the examination, he was conscious of being the single blonde head in a sea of black. Thus he became the first Caucasian to pass the stiff Japanese Medical Board requirements.[5] In fact all of these events had happened so fast that within a week of his arrival (January 1, 1956) Richard was able to consult on a difficult surgery case.

As the "new family" arriving in Tokyo, Richard and Carol naturally wanted to make a good first-impression. They started inauspiciously when nine-year-old Carol and her brother Jerry, along with one of their new classmates, locked their teacher in the schoolroom. It took her some time to get herself out.

The kids' knew that punishment was inevitable. Very much his father's son, Father Richard inquired, "So how many times should I spank your little bottoms?"

With the heroic integrity of the family into which he had been born, Jerry volunteered, "We'll take five."

After the affair was over, Carol—also within in the range of rational family attitudes—turned on her brother in a rage. "You could have said one or two, and that would have worked just as well!"

Further on the domestic front, all four adult Nelsons worked on a fascinating match-making project. Misako worked for Richard and Carol in Tokyo and became a beloved member of the household. Because everyone else spoke fluent Japanese, her English, remained very poor. One Christmas someone gave Richard a bottle of Old Spice aftershave. Immediately thereafter it disappeared, and no one could figure out where it had gone. Months later, Carol discovered it right where it was supposed to be, in a kitchen cupboard among the rest of the spice jars.

Meanwhile, Andrew Nelson decided that Miki Kita, an American Japanese bachelor living in Colorado, would make a good pen pal for Misako. Miki Kita was an x-ray technician at Porter Sanitarium in Denver. Rather shortly the correspondence turned into real love letters. In complete trust, Misako asked Carol to help her write letters to her as-yet-unseen suitor. In time, Carol obliged. "But I almost felt that I myself was having an affair with Miki Kita."

When the couple agreed that they wanted to marry, Andrew Nelson made all of the arrangements for the would-be bridegroom to come to Tokyo. These arrangements didn't seem peculiar to anyone. Nobody, however, had really foreseen the depth of cultural differences and the confusion that could arise.

Carol counseled Misako about her bridegroom's arrival. "Miki Kita has grown up in America, so don't be surprised if he gives you a little kiss." That didn't happen.

As they all returned home from the ship dock, the young people sat far apart, each pressed up to an opposite window in the back seat. Miki Kita expressed surprise that his betrothed could write English so well. Carol tried to explain, but with little success.

Once at the house, Richard and his wife immediately went out to visit friends so that Miki Kita and Misako could be alone and get better acquainted. They returned a couple of hours later to find a nervous and confused bride-to-be sitting alone in the living room.

"But all I said was, 'Why don't you put on your *yukata* (pajamas)?' He didn't want to, but when he finally did, he just went to his bed."

Alas! In Japan everyone knew that at the end of the day it was the custom to put on your *yukata* (lounging *kimono*) to relax and visit in the evening. The upright and mystified Miki Kita, once in his pajamas, however, understood that he had nowhere to go but bed.

Wise and gracious as all of the Nelsons were, even they couldn't foresee every breakdown of communication that would occur before this "cross-cultural" Japanese couple they'd sponsored would marry and launch into a happy family life.

In the main, after a six-year absence, Andrew could make an insightful assessment of the post-war climate in Japan. Despite the "noisy communists," he observed very little resentment against the United States. At the same time, officials saw American movies as contributing to the moral depravity of Japan's youth. The country's long history of courtesy was becoming besmirched by gangs, gamblers, drug dealers--all bent on violence. In fact, it used to be "a constant joy to live among a people who, decade in and decade out, were uniformly considerate of others."

Now, Andrew sighed, "Something has happened." People are mistaking "liberty for license," as the Japanese public returned to material interests. Suicide was more prevalent than ever. Nonetheless, the "freedom of religion" held in place, and Nelson remained convinced that Christian missions had a unique opportunity for success.

At the same time, evangelism had changed. Presenting the Voice of Prophecy program in the Japanese language had, in a short time, very gratifying results. After his escape from Los Banos Camp at the end of World War II, Paul Eldridge had coached the Kings Heralds and Del Delker to sing in Japanese. That effort was so successful that listeners in Japan couldn't believe that those fine singers were not Japanese. Enrollments came in at about 400 per month, and attendance at evangelistic efforts improved. By November 1953 the VOP had 18,828 graduates and 1,735 baptisms.[6]

Andrew always had a special concern for his beloved college in Naraha. It had been used as a Japanese army medical training unity. Although it had not been bombed, it had been badly used and—like Philippine Union College—needed repair. The farmland had been depleted of its nutritive value, the library had been looted, and valuable shop machinery had been sold.

Nonetheless, all was well. Andrew and Vera were back home in Japan, and they had much work to do. Both felt the assurance of being exactly where God wanted them to be.

[1] Arturo G. Macasiano, "How the Site for Mountain View College, Philippines, Was Found," *Review and Herald* (June 156, 1972), pp. 12-13.

[2] In 1970 Andrew Nelson himself helped pack two telescopes for Mountain View College, gifts of Dr. Marion Barnard.

[3] See a history of Mountain View College in Mindanao, Philippines. Irene Wakeham-Lee, *The Mountain, the View, and the College* (National City, CA: ValMar Grapics, Inc., 2003)

[4] Andrew Nelson liked to say: "Variety is as restful to the mind as standing on the left leg after being long on the right."

[5] With the signing of the Peace Treaty, the Japanese insisted that these important medical examinations be conducted in their local language. Ichimura became a translator and teacher of Japanese at Japan Missionary College.

[6] In general, baptisms remained about 300 per year.

19. Still on the College Circuit

In 1958 the Nelsons returned to the Philippines. This time, in a complete role-reversal. Andrew served as the Dean of Philippine Union College with Dr. Manalaysay as president. No problem. "It is a joy to be working with Dr. Manalaysay again," Nelson declared.

Meanwhile, Vera broke her arm and was much less useful than she wanted to be in the business of getting settled again into their campus home. Otherwise, their return to PUC bore no trace of the heartache that attended their departure five years earlier.

With his usual zest, Andrew took up his teaching again. The Graduate School, happily, had forty-four students for summer school. He noted proudly that the students who came from other parts of the Orient regularly returned to their home fields, carrying their expertise with them. At that point in time, only one student had gone to the United States. "We can save them for the work [out here]." Nelson had an in-depth vision of higher education for the Philippines.

Although he returned to find that hopes of moving PUC to a new location had fallen through—again—the necessity remained. "We cannot carry out the program of Christian education in its fullness here. The influence of Baesa (the "ghetto" outside of the PUC compound walls) is very, very detrimental."

Currently, a prospective piece of land near Lucena was under consideration. It had all of the characteristics he looked for in his long-standing move-the-college agenda. As it turned out, this prospect would also fail, and the actual re-location of Philippine Union College was, sadly, still many years in the future.

Meanwhile, Mountain View College was prospering. Andrew hailed as a very good thing the arrival of the first "permanent president," Todd Murdoch, a Scotsman from Canadian Union College in Western Canada.

When he visited the campus, Nelson viewed a very material fulfillment of his dream for the Bukidnon Project. "The college is in shipshape condition with the lawns mowed, peanuts and all the vegetables looking just right, all machineries and equipment humming, the cowboys attending the cattle in the fields, and the cleanliness and orderliness of the campus—100%."

Andrew could not have been more pleased. Thanks to the engineering skills of the redoubtable Dr. William Richli the sawmill was humming along on the hydroelectric plant he'd set up. Free power for the whole campus! Dr. Harry Miller donated a factory for making soymilk, another by-product of the farm.

The next year MVC sent two urgent calls for Nelson to come as Dean. Although he would have very much liked that appointment, PUC wasn't willing to release him. In any case, he was able to thoroughly enjoy the Week of Prayer he conducted at MVC that year. He had nothing but praise for the way Murdoch had shaped up the college. He basked in the compliments that came in from all sides. "It is the best example of a community school. It is truly giving the Filipino people an education that will help to build the economy of the country, because of the work-study program." The 600 students had a "fine spirit." They were looking forward to installing a telescope on a hill that they'd set aside for that specific purpose. Also Princess Plang was contributing several thousand rubber-tree plants to create a new industry.

Best of all, the Nelsons heard words of appreciation on all sides. "The Lord marvelously used you in providing for the youth of the Philippines." "Thank you for your dream and foresight." Yes, "MVC is the School of the Prophets in these modern times."

One more time, the South Philippine Union Mission Committee asked Andrew Nelson to become the Academic Dean at MVC. Although he could not accept the invitation, the fact that the call had been made three times was comfort enough. His service in the Far Eastern Division had now come full circle. Japan to the Philippines. Then Japan to the Philippines a second time. Now it was time to go home—this time on PR (Permanent Return).

The year 1960 might have been another furlough year for Andrew and Vera Nelson, but this time it would be different. They'd given more than forty years of service to the church. A new administrative regulation required "that missionaries returning after age sixty-five are to stay home." For many of the pioneers this was a painful order to obey. "These years of mission service," Andrew mused, "have gone by almost like a flash. . . .They have been very interesting but very strenuous years."

This time the Nelsons' home-going journey held no surprises, just the pleasure of leisure time with friends and family. They left Manila on June 9 and made Japan their first stop. Son Richard's family was there. Not unexpectedly, Andrew found saying farewell to Japan was the most difficult part of cutting his ties with the Orient. While in Tokyo, he appeared on the NHK-TV weekly program called "*My Secret*." On that occasion fifteen of "his" former prisoners-of-war in Bilibid came in person to greet him.

In India they spent time with Andrew's brother Philip and his wife Ruby. Dr. Philip was the medical Secretary for the Southern Asia Division, and he was Medical Director at the large sanitarium in Nuzvid. Some of the medical practice puzzled Andrew. Patients at death's door, for instance, might be removed from expert medical care, often for little reason. Then they could die or be left to the often questionable treatments of a local practitioner. Sometimes the latter burned them with irons so that a new and greater pain would take their minds off of the original pain of their illness. To Andrew's busy, rational mind these cases were utterly frustrating. "Can't something be done about this?"

In Beirut, Lebanon, their daughter Dorothy and her husband Kenneth Oster were teaching at Middle East College. They showed them the best of the Middle East, from the pyramids of Egypt to the ruins of Babylon in Iraq. "No man even pitches his tent there . . . [and] desert creatures will lie there" (Isaiah 13:20)," Andrew recalled, but they did catch a glimpse of a single fox slinking around in the mud-brick debris.

The last stops of the "Grand Tour" toward home were to visit cousins in Sweden and the Northern European Division office in Edgware, England.[1]

Yes, this was, indeed, Permanent Return, but in no way did that mean idleness. Andrew cheerfully took up the invitation to join the faculty at La Sierra College in Southern California. His "prescribed" retirement had come with honors. In recognition of his life-long contributions to the cause of education, the Board of Trustees unanimously voted him the faculty status of Emeritus Professor of Educational Foundations.[2]

Andrew described himself as "a retired volunteer." He was

heard to say, "Well, the brethren wanted us to retire, so we got that over with." That chore completed he was then free to get on with the rest of his life. Happily, he had a considerable amount of work left to do. For Andrew Nelson retiring was simply a "re-tread," and he was ready for the open road again.

In August, 1961, Andrew and Vera Nelson settled on Peacock Lane in La Sierra and joined the college community.[3] Once again, he took up his favorite mode of teaching—without exams or formal grades. For his education class, he used the compilation he'd put together while teaching at Philippine Union College, "The Gist of Christian Education."

When Andrew addressed the college administrators, academy principals, and education secretaries at a large Council, he felt comfortably secure on "home ground." The topic? "The Curriculum for a Seventh-day Adventist School." Moreover, he "was asked to feel unhampered by what our schools may be doing at the present time." Instead, he was encouraged to "line up a program based entirely on the Spirit of Prophecy plan." A task that he pursued with zest.

Andrew Nelson had been a long-time proponent of research, especially in a senior college. His dictionary work, of course, lent credence to his ideas. "My dictionary has been well received and has become the standard in twenty-five universities and forty-five high schools where Japanese is taught." This publicity opened the way for him to communicate with other scholars he met at conventions and thus put La Sierra College "on the map."

Andrew was delighted when the College purchased a twelve-inch telescope for a bargain of $3,750. (It retailed for $7,000.) He had been instrumental in getting a twelve-inch telescope as a gift apiece for both Japan Missionary College and Philippine Union College. He had always felt "that astronomy is the most important science," and he longed to give students an "opportunity to look beyond this sin-cursed world into the sinless and glorious expanses of God's tremendous universe."

Beyond the classroom duties Andrew's calendar was full. In the summer he traveled as a field representative for the college. "My correspondence with parents and students in the field results in bringing in many students and also in holding [them]." Often, he was the first person people wanted to see when they arrived on campus.

Over the years, Andrew became a favorite advisor to foreign students. The average ran from about 175 students from approximately thirty-five countries. These responsibilities gave him good reason to revisit the Philippines. (He spent five days at PUC and two at MVC.[4]) By keeping in touch with the mission fields he also became an advisor to prospective missionaries. At the same time, he spent hours at personal counseling with other young people who just needed to talk, something he considered "very important."

Naturally, Andrew's fame as a linguist had preceded him. Soon he was involved in a Navajo language school at Monument Valley Mission Hospital. Astonished colleagues questioned him as he headed off to New Mexico. "How can you do that when you don't even know any Navajo?"

"I can teach any language in the world without knowing it," he replied. "All languages are alike. I plan to use Navajo Indian assistants who actually will start the class talking." From there, he explained, they would follow his directions in developing the course. He would then confer with them between each of the classes. The method would emphasize conversation in the new language. That is where it all started. Eighteen Loma Linda University doctors, dentists, and nurses doing mission work among the Navajo Indians took the course. Nelson sat in with the students, learning as they did.

"The Navajo language is rather difficult," he admitted. "But it's the language of 120,000 people, and those people must be reached."

Smiling, Nelson remembered something else from World War II. "Navajos in the U. S. military spoke their language in code," he said, with satisfaction. "That's why the Japanese never could decipher it—and break our code."

During his second summer in Southern California, Andrew was active in the "experimental project" of Sierra Ranch School for Boys in Arizona. The summer camp had been set up along Nelson's triple program for education—"Mental, Physical and Spiritual." It had all of the earmarks of Nelson's basic educational plan.[5] One student characterized the plan as:

> Study hard when you study.
> Work hard when you work.
> Play hard when you play.
> Eat hard when you eat.
> Rest hard when you rest.

Regular campfire worships were held in their own "Forest Cathedral Church" that the boys created themselves. Nelson spent a week out on this 472-acre ranch. Those who were there remembered that his "buoyant courage and sense of humor" really made the camp "work."[6]

Andrew enjoyed all of this work so much that he hardly remembered—nor did anyone else notice—that he'd really retired!

[1] *Northern Light* (August, 1961).

[2] The La Sierra College yearbook, *Meteor,* was dedicated to him for his "deep interest in the students, his devotion to the maintenance of principles of Christian education, and for his life of service to his fellowmen and to God."

[3] "La Sierra College: Dr. A. N. Nelson Joins Faculty." *Pacific Union Recorder* (January 23, 1961), p. 16.

[4] "Former PUC President Visits Manila." *Far Eastern Division Outlook* (September, 1971), p. 12.

[5] *Pacific Union Recorder* (September 14, 1964), p. 1. The Ranch program called for: Morning study; dinner and rest until 1.30 p.m.; three-hour work period (in groups of five, each led by a teacher); doing one's own laundry, and taking turns with kitchen duty.

[6] *Pacific Union Recorder* (February 14, 1964), p. 1; (September 14, 1964), p. 1.

20. Retirement Assignments

One task that never ended for Andrew was visiting churches, preaching and giving mission talks.[1] The record of his "off campus" enterprises is a long one. He was always available for weekend speaking appointments. He never tired of preaching the gospel—and of preaching it to foreign people in faraway places.

In May 1963 one mission field event drove itself home to the Andrew Nelsons with staggering pain. A terror beyond imagining. His brother Philip and wife Ruby had delayed their permanent return for a year, waiting for a replacement doctor to arrive in Nuzvid, India. Finally, they loaded their luggage into their little Fiat car and headed for Delhi and the plane that would take them home.

About noon they had a flat tire. Phil got the spare on, and an hour later another tire blew out. What to do? He had to take a passing truck to Allahabad to buy two new tires. He looked at the lowering sun and then at his watch, 4:15 p.m. The nearby village appeared comfortable enough. This was just a nuisance—nothing more.

"Bye, bye. I'll wait for you here," Ruby cheerfully called after him as he climbed aboard the rattling, overloaded truck. That was the last time he would hear her voice.

It was after 9 p.m. before Phil could get back. The car had been ransacked and Ruby was gone. "Ruby, my darling, where are you," he cried. He heard only the hiss of a departing dust storm. No reply.

The trucker who had brought him from town searched with his flashlight. Then they found her. Some seventy-five feet from the car, she lay lifeless on the bank of a little pond, her throat cut. Crazed with grief and chilled with shock, Philip prayed through the rest of the night, lying beside her.

With all of the clarity of hindsight, everyone in the entire mission family around India learned the lesson. What should the Nelsons have done? If they had walked to that little village and asked for Ruby to be guarded, she would have been safe. The ancient laws of hospitality would have guaranteed her life. But out there in the beautiful "outback" of India who could have foreseen such horror that afternoon?

After Ruby was buried in Poona, Philip was detained until the attackers were arrested. During that time he visited five of the murderers on death row. He was able to forgive them, as they waited for the gallows.[2] He returned home to re-build a family practice and renew his life in Ceres, near Modesto, California.

The Nelson family closed its ranks, and life went on.

Above all, Andrew never lost sight of his many years in the Far East nor of his intense concern for all things Japanese. Soon after his arrival at La Sierra College, his name appeared on the roster of a dozen distinguished guests attending the Japanese Camp Meeting at Wawona, Yosemite. The 275 attendees came from seven Japanese churches on the West Coast.[3] Then, he joined a "snow trip to the Big Pines area" with the West Los Angeles Japanese-American Church.[4] One year, an invitation to speak at a Week of Prayer at Canadian Union College in Alberta, Canada, also opened the way to speak at the Japanese church in British Columbia.

On their return trip to California the Nelsons stopped by to visit the "1208 Relatives." The original home of Anders and Gustava Nelson on 1208 Shelby Street in Seattle had long since become the center for family events for many generations.[5] After it was sold in the 1940s, however, gatherings had to be held elsewhere.

Andrew and Vera accounted their 50th wedding anniversary "a wonderful affair," staged by their two daughters-in-law, Carol and Arlene. Dorothy and Kenneth Oster came all the way in from Michigan. Andrew's special contribution was to announce that he was taking his bride on a ten-day honeymoon trip to Hawaii, a place she'd never visited. Of course, on the side, he gave a lecture at the University of Hawaii and undertook various church appointments. He'd long ago learned where to place family priorities, however, and the couple thoroughly enjoyed their Hawaiian "get away" that year (1967).

One day in 1970 a unique visitor showed up in Nelson's office at La Sierra College. Jacob Mittleider turned out to be an international consultant who had developed some new ideas about making agriculture production more effective. Always interested in good farming for schools, Andrew listened intently. Mittleider had experimented with scientific gardening and farming in Okinawa[6] and had "developed methods that," he said, "might combat world starvation." This was an idea broad enough to catch the undivided attention of Andrew Nelson. It was a grand design to help mankind alleviate (or eliminate) hunger.

"There are nearly seven billion people in the world, and half of them are malnourished or go to bed hungry each night. I maintain," Mittleider went on, "that the land we have for agriculture is capable of producing enough food to feed all of these people and to give them a wholesome, well-balanced diet. Think of how world health would improve even if our population shot up to 30 billion!"

Actually, he'd thought of everything—the scientific use of existing farmlands as well as the most efficient means of storing, transporting, and marketing surpluses. He had even worked on the land at one of Nelson's favorite projects, Mountain View College in the Philippines.

"You ought to write a book about this fantastic method of gardening," Andrew Nelson urged, fired up by the idea.

"Oh, but writing books is not my talent," Mittleider replied. "I'm sure of that."

"All right," Nelson announced. "It's done. I'll write the book, and you provide the contents for it." It took about ten hours a day for the next two years to complete the work, but *Food for Everyone* came out in 1973. Subsequently it was translated into Japanese and Spanish.[7]

"The Mittleider Method" appealed to both the home gardener and the serious farmer. As usual, the new, provocative ideas met with resistance. Here Nelson could speak from long experience. "One thing I've learned and found very helpful is this," he told his new partner, Jacob Mittleider. (By now Nelson had truly mastered the arts of leadership.) "I decided to talk over plans in the formative stages to give my associates the opportunity to ask questions and make some contributions. Then when we went ahead, everyone felt that it was their plan. In my early days, I worked out the plans all by myself in great detail and then just announced them to my faculty. But I finally learned that this is not the best way."

Mittleider took this wisdom of Andrew Nelson to heart and was thus better able to cope with criticism that met his radically new farming methodology. Without question his program resulted in excellent produce. While the Mittleider Method soil analysis and nurturing remains useful in American "factory farming," it proved not to be sustainable in Third World countries. To what purpose is a mountain of beautiful, near-perfect carrots in Africa where the population cannot pay the price for building up their garden soil? Perhaps the people have not even been trained yet to *eat* a fresh diet. For them, simple composting is actually a much less expensive way for treating the ground.

At the General Conference session in Atlanta in 1970 the Nelsons had a family time. Ken Oster purchased a six-passenger trailer for the occasion. It comfortably and economically housed himself and Dorothy, his mother, and Andrew and Vera Nelson.

Ken and Dorothy had been spending all of their furloughs studying at Andrews University. Now Ken had received his fourth degree from that institution. Soon he would be returning to Lebanon, ready to break through the wall of Islam with the Five-Day Plan to Stop Smoking. Dorothy had completed her MMus in organ performance under Dr. Warren Becker. Upon their return, she would play an organ concert in the Middle East College chapel on an organ that she and Ken had built themselves.[8] Resourcefulness was pretty much a given throughout the Nelson family.

Andrew Nelson had his own project to pursue at the Atlanta General Conference session. *Food for Everyone* was hot off the press, so he could promote it and the Mittleider program up and down the crowded aisles at the Convention Center.

Best of all, his retirement years gave Andrew a chance to pay attention to his dictionaries. He put the finishing touches on what proved to be his masterpiece, *The Modern Reader's Japanese-English Character Dictionary*, first published in 1962.

Having been a student of the Japanese language for fifty-five years, his work could hardly be improved upon. Although a revised and computerized edition (prepared by a team at the University of Hawaii) appeared in 1997, many scholars have continued to prefer Nelson's original work. It simply worked better for people struggling with the complexities of *Kanji*, and it remains the standard for universities worldwide, wherever Japanese is taught.

Andrew Nelson received due honors for his remarkable work as a lexicographer.[9] His *Japanese-English Dictionary of Technical Terms* contained 150,000 terms and was republished in many languages, including Russian. He produced his *Japanese-English Supplementary*

Dictionary during his wartime service in the United States Army.

In November 1972, Andrew and Vera were on leave from Loma Linda University and were working at the South China Adventist College in Hong Kong. They were invited to attend the Annual Council in Singapore.

On Sabbath afternoon in the college auditorium on Upper Serangoon Road, Dr. Charles B. Hirsch led out in a celebration of "A Century of Adventist World Education." Sitting modestly at the back, the Nelsons were suddenly ordered to the front. Dr. Hirsch slipped a broad blue ribbon over Andrew's head. Attached was the Medallion of Merit, the highest award given by the General Conference Department of Education.

"A veteran educator and long-time missionary in the Far East" with forty years of service—the honor was richly deserved. Nonetheless, Andrew was visibly surprised.[10]

Actually, no one had ever before seen him so taken off his guard. Habitually, the "old warrior" was always planning the "Next Big Thing" and spent very little time on what had already passed.

[1] *Pacific Union Recorder* (October 2, 1961), p. 13; (February 19, 1962), p. 6; Nelson recounted the Bilibid story at Glendale Church on (February 10, 1962), p. 6.
[2] On January 1, 1967, the Ruby Nelson Memorial Hospital was officially established in Jalandhar, Punjab, India. It is a 52-bed institution. See. *Southern Asia Tidings* (February, 1967), p. 19. Ruby Nelson's murderers were executed in 1965.
[3] Harold Kona, "Pacific Union Japanese Camp Meeting." *Pacific Union Recorder* (September 23, 1963), p. 1.
[4] *Pacific Union Recorder* (March 12, 1962), p. 13.
[5] Andrew Nelson carefully recorded five weddings he had performed for members of the 1208 Family: His brother Reuben and Fay Nelson, his daughter Dorothy and Kenneth Oster, his brother Philip and Lorene Nelson, his granddaughter Rae and Sidney Kettner, and his sister Vivian and Lester Cushman. He also noted that the 1208 Family had been missionaries in ten countries: Japan, China, Philippines, Hong Kong, Iran, Lebanon, India, Bolivia, Ethiopia, and Guam.
[6] In Okinawa the High Commissioner and University President visited Mittleider's farm. They especially admired the way he could make his own soil. Mittleider had lectured on college campuses in the USA and abroad. In New Guinea on only nine acres of land they grew enough surplus in the first year to earn over $3,200. His other international endeavors included Fiji and Tanzania.
[7] "Dr. A. N. Nelson Co-Authors Book *Food for Everyone*." *Pacific Union Recorder* (August 6, 1973), p. 8. The book was printed by Walla Walla Press, 1973.
[8] The Osters ordered a Schober organ kit to take back with them to their mission field. Ken did the woodwork for the organ and Dorothy installed the electronic parts. The construction job took them about 300 hours of work.
[9] "Dr. Andrew Nelson Receives Honor." *Pacific Union Recorder* (December 3, 1973), p.7.
[10] Retha H. Eldridge, "Report of the Far Eastern Division Annual Council" (Singapore, December, 1972), p. 7.

21. The Full Circle

Andrew had one more scholarly project. One that he had first glimpsed thirty years earlier. That was the tumultuous year he spent in Shanghai before the Pacific War closed down the entire Far East.

In 1971 he decided to create a Chinese dictionary. He found a collaborator in young Dr. Wilbur Nelson at the Loma Linda School of Public Health. He envisioned "The Modern Reader's Chinese-English Character Dictionary" as a worthy companion volume for his *Japanese Character Dictionary* already famous around the world. Besides, this would be his personal contribution to the evangelizing of China.

A crew of seven—a Mandarin scholar and six student researchers–were at work in Hong Kong, and Andrew very much wanted to be with them. Before he could plan a journey he had a fainting spell. For a few days he was laid up, under the watchful eye of his son, Dr. Richard. "Look, Dad, you've had a stroke. A mild one, but still a stroke. Why don't you just forget about going to Hong Kong now? The Chinese dictionary can wait."

Time passed, and Andrew felt perfectly well. Eighty-years old? No matter, he had things to tend to. He planned a five or six month absence from La Sierra. Vera couldn't come immediately, but he'd manage. There was, in fact, no stopping him. His physician son detected some other health problems, but he decided they could wait. So after the manner of most of the children of ambitious parents, Richard let his father go.

In that winter of 1975 Andrew had been devoting every spare moment to the big Chinese dictionary project. The two Dr. Nelsons were looking forward to a publication date in 1976.

Once ready to go Andrew added several more items to his itinerary. First, he had to stop in Japan to visit his old friends there.

Also, he had to settle some publication problems concerning the revised printing of his Japanese dictionary. At the same time, he found a publisher for his Japanese translation of the Mittleider book. Next came Korea and a visit with new missionaries, his niece and nephew, Mitzi and Jerry Wiggle, the Korean Union treasurer. Okinawa was a required stop also because he wanted to know how the Mittleider program was progressing there.

Finally settled at the college in Kowloon, Andrew took up a teaching load comprised of his favorite subjects: Principles of Seventh-day Adventist Education, Advanced English Conversation, History of Education, and Methods of Teaching a Foreign Language. (He put in at least ten classroom hours a week.) "There's quite an interest here in teaching the Japanese language," he wrote. The new hospital was attracting Japanese patients, and "it would [be] helpful if the nurses could speak the Japanese language." Yes, he could teach an extra language class too!

When he first arrived in Hong Kong—alone—Andrew promptly fell into a decline. Vera's good vegetarian cooking had always kept him and the family healthy. Left on his own, he had a hard time at the college cafeteria. White rice and "slim side dishes" three times a day began to drag him down. "I soon got so weak that I could hardly puff up the stairs to the campus," he complained. Things got even worse when he tried to make his own meals. "Remember," he told himself, "You're now among the elderly and the aged. You can't last forever." "So," he explained, "I decided to look for a cemetery."

Then one day "two angelic student missionaries," Bob and Anne Fetrick, appeared on his doorstep. "We're taking over. You're eating with us from now on." They came in "loaded with dishes of delicious, nutritious food."

At about the same time, Dr. Sid Kettner at the Stubbs Road Hospital also intervened. "He discovered that I was low on hemoglobin and loaded me up with iron tablets and shot me with more iron in my arm." The doctor's wife Rae was Andrew's own granddaughter, so he enjoyed their company. He especially liked the times that involved sailing with them on their "junk" (a Chinese style sail boat) out on the bay.

Soon Andrew felt like himself again, and he "officially" removed himself from the roster of "the aged." He also stopped looking for a cemetery and was in pretty good shape when Vera arrived a few weeks later and resumed the management of his private life.

In any case, whatever his situation, the Chinese Dictionary was never far from Andrew's mind. Because he felt that relations with China were improving, he predicted that "our dictionary will fill a big need." Meanwhile, Dr. Lin Yutang had just brought a huge Chinese-English Character Dictionary. Andrew wrote an official review for it. He found it a "splendid, conservative dictionary" and a "grand . . . climax to a long series of Chinese-English character dictionaries."

Still, he did not feel threatened in the least by this enormous book. (It was selling for the staggering price of $40.00!) In contrast, the entries in the Nelson dictionary would be rendered in the "new simplified Peking character forms," and each one would have the full Chinese character accompanying it. Independent cross-reference entries would also accompany each character. The book would be slim and efficient.

Moreover, Nelson's dictionary would "cover all vocabulary." Everything–"conservative Taiwan, Peking political terms, Seventh-day-Adventist work, Catholic and/or Protestant words, and modern newspaper and magazine terms." Andrew expected that his "invention of how to find characters more easily" would be a real asset for students of Chinese.

Wilbur Nelson, Andrew's associate, had earned a doctorate in Chinese culture. He and Chinese students had already, as early as September 1964, finished the primary carding of 140,000 modern Chinese words. With his usual obsession with thoroughness, however, Andrew had to be sure that all of the important characters would be in the dictionary and all cross-referenced. That meant, "combing through literature, books, glossaries, magazines, and newspapers." Moreover, they would use the new pronunciations. So, Andrew concluded in a monumental understatement, "there's more work to be done."

Presently, Andrew and Vera Nelson were invited up from Hong Kong to attend the 50th Anniversary celebrations at Japan Union College (May 2-5, 1975). Seeing Yokohama Harbor on a foggy morning threw him into nostalgic recollections of their arrival in that same place on another rainy morning fifty-three years earlier. A torrent of images surged through his mind: The ship sailings, the arrival of their "triplet" children, happy summers at Nojiri and Karuizawa, and all of the familiar landmarks on the old Naraha campus.

Now his beloved school was about to move again. The

selling price for the Naraha property had proved to be so high that the Mission now could afford to start all over again, with new buildings to replace the tired old originals. Nelson pronounced the new site "very good" with "lovely gardens, seventy-five acres, and nice hills for boundaries."

Six of the eleven presidents of Japan Missionary College, *Nihon Saniku Gakuin*, were present for the Golden Anniversary celebrations. The Nelsons met many old friends from the founding days of the campus.

No one, of course, knew more history than Andrew did. His recollections read like a textbook. He spoke of William C. Grainger who opened the "Japanese-English Bible School" in Tokyo in 1898. Eighty students came out, he said, and that school was conducted "much like our modern language schools."

After the Naraha property was purchased in 1926, the Tokyo Boys School moved out to the country. Andrew ruefully recalled how his crew of eager amateurs built the woodshop in one day, and how it fell down the very next day. Humbly, they then requested the services of a "real builder." That was Mr. Myron Powers. After the closure during the war years, the college became co-educational with the Girls School moving to Naraha in 1947. Now, half a century later, the enrollment stood at 550 students.

In his usual good form, Andrew Nelson preached the Sabbath sermon that weekend. In Japanese of course. After all, he'd studied the Japanese language for fifty-five years. Plaques and special honors were distributed to former presidents and teachers, all in the gracious manner that the Japanese know so well.[1]

When the Nelsons departed for Hong Kong after those joyful days of fellowship, no one could know that this would be Andrew's last public meeting. Once back in Hong Kong he immediately returned to work on his Chinese dictionary. He and his scholars expected to publish it within three years (1978), and the task loomed large over them all.

On Wednesday evening, May 7, he attended a social gathering with his student-staff. He thoroughly enjoyed chatting with his fellow-workers. Relaxed and cheerful, he laughed as jokes and light chatter rippled round the room.

As it turned out, that gathering was Andrew Nelson's farewell party. An hour later, as he prepared to go to bed, he found that he couldn't turn on the water to wash his face. Then he fell to the bathroom floor, unconscious. This time the stroke—which was a massive one—did not reverse itself. He died on May 17, 1975.[2]

Richard and his brother Donald immediately sent an air ticket for Dorothy to fly to Hong Kong to be with her mother. Ten days of loving care and prayers surrounded his bed in the hospital, but Andrew never came out of his coma.

Burying him right at his post of duty where he fell might have been a natural decision. His daughter Dorothy discovered, however, that a burial plot was guaranteed for only seven years before it was discarded. (Andrew Nelson would not have approved of that kind of instability.) Therefore she and her mother decided to be practical.

Andrew was cremated and carried home as hand luggage. He would have liked to go that way. Quietly, decisively, rationally, and with dignity. Just three days later, Andrew's old friend, Victor Armstrong, died in Portland, Oregon. It was as if the two stalwarts of Adventism in Japan just went away together.

Back home, on the evening of May 20, 1975, Loma Linda University honored Andrew Nelson at a memorial service in the La Sierra Church. Tributes came from the University President, fellow-Scandinavian V. Norskov Olsen, and from representatives of the Far Eastern Division, along with music by the John T. Hamilton Chorale.

Andrew would have been sorry for just one thing. No one remained who could carry on the demanding work on the Chinese dictionary, so it never became a reality. Certainly it would go against everything in Andrew Nelson's nature to leave a job unfinished. Still, if it weren't the dictionary, it would have been something else. Some project that would have consumed his mind and heart to his last hour.

[1] "Japan College Marks Golden Anniversary." *Far Eastern Division Outlook* (July, 1975), p. 8.
[2] *Review and Herald* (June 5, 1975), p. 32. "Andrew Nelson Passes Away in Hong Kong," *Pacific Union Recorder* (May 24, 1975), p. 8.

EPILOGUE

This book goes to press in 2010, thirty-five years after Andrew Nelson died. We have had a year not only of financial turmoil but also of environmental disasters. Earthquakes, tornadoes, floods, and tsunamis, almost beyond count.

Then, in March came the eruption of the Eyjafjallajokull volcano in Iceland. Instantaneously, it snarled up air traffic all over Europe and, ultimately, throughout the world. People became enraged, but there was no one to blame. It's as if God looked down upon us, enmeshed in our high technology, confident in our own abilities, and so smug in our arrogance. He said, "Um! Let Me show you a little thing here. Just a small volcano on this island."

Andrew Nelson would have observed this unstoppable cosmic power and said, "Yes, of course. That's my God at work, allowing these natural events to happen."

Then Andrew could have looked upon our large church organization—the hospitals, the schools, and all the rest. After all, he gave his whole life to Christian education, and he had passion for learning.

He would have said, "Yes, that's an admirable system that God helped us create. Our access to knowledge has no boundaries. I see that my God is there also."

Then he would remember that ghastly, gloomy night at Bilibid Prison when, one by one, he walked those Japanese prisoners-of-war to their execution. He knew each one who had found life in Christ. For them the hangman's rope was but a temporary transition.

Andrew Nelson would have said, "Ah! That's my God too, right inside a man's heart. I know. That's the way He leads each one of us, all the way into His kingdom."

The Nelson Family Tree[1]

Anders/Andrew Alexander (Swanstrom) Nelson[2]
Of Janstorp, Staffanstorp, Vimmerby, Sweden & Great Falls MT, Seattle WA, USA.
(1865-1948)

+ (1891)

Gustava Caroline Jonson[3]
Of Byrnakulla, Astorp, Helsingborg, Sweden & Kansas City, MO, Great Falls MT, Seattle WA, USA.
(1866-1931)

Andrew Nathaniel Nelson
(1893 –1975)
+ (Mar 24, 1918)
Vera Elizabeth Shoff
(1893-1984)
1. Richard Andrew Nelson
(1920-)
2. Donald George Nelson
(1922-)
3. Dorothy Gertrude Nelson
(1922-)

Gertrude Katherine
(1897-1978)
+ (1921)
(1) George C. Bergman, Jr.
(1899-1957)
1. George Clyde Bergman
(1924-)
2. Phyllis Vivian Nelson-Bergman
(1930-)
3. Janet Gertrude Bergman
(1936-1967)
+ (1972)
(2) Henry Ward Martin
(1898-1983)

Philip Swaney
(1899-1985)
+ (1927)
(1) Ruby Eltina Gil
(1903-1964)
1. Martin Gill Nelson
(1931-)
2. Philip Sidney
(1937-1999)
3. William Lee Thomas
(1938-)
+ (1966)
(2) Margaret Lorene Ausherman
(1910-)

Reuben Emmanuel
(1901-2004)
+ (1925)
(1) Fay M. Stokes
(1902-1989)
1. Robert Lamont Nelson
(1934-)
2. Marilyn Fay Nelson
(1938-)
+ (1990)
(2) Ellen Waddell
(1912-)

Olivia (Vivian) Elizabeth
(1907-2008)
+1931 (div 1945)
(1) Elwyn Smith
(1904-1961)
1. Mitzi Lois Smith
(1932)
2. William Orville Smith
(1940-)
+ (1967)
(2) Lester Harvey Cushman
(1904-1981)

[1] As of 2010, Dr. Andrew Nathaniel and Vera Nelson had 90 direct descendants. He worked out his own family numbering scheme that conforms to no known genealogical format. With himself as #1 he nurtured much family solidarity, and each member is jealously proud of his or her own number. See Vivian Nelson-Smith-Cushman, *Stories from the Family of 1208* (Lincoln, NE, 2006). Published by Jerry and Mitzi Wiggle, P. O. Box 66, Bennet, NE, 68317. (jerrywiggle@yahoo.com)

[2] **Andrew Alexander Nelson** (1865-1948) left Sweden as Anders Swanstrom. He Anglicized his name and added his middle name when he became a U. S. citizen. His grandmother, Kjerstin Andersdottir, married her aged foster father to retain a piece of property in Sweden. His father Nils took his stepfather's name, Swanstrom. With the exception of Jons, Andrew's siblings assumed the name of Nelson when they emigrated to America.

[3] **Gustava Caroline Jonson** (1866-1930) was the daughter of Assrina Bengstad (of Byrnakulla) and John Oberg (of Astorp). Her mother had another daughter, Christina, who was about six years older than Gustava. All three women worked as *pigas* (housemaids), the only occupation open to them. Most of the Swedes emigrating to America were from the working class. They had the most reason to leave their homeland. As the Nelson story reveals, Gustava and her family burned out to be a bundle of talent and ambition, just waiting for a chance to achieve.

The Andrew N. Nelson Family

Andrew Nathaniel Nelson (1893-1975)   +Mar 24, 1918   **Vera Elizabeth Shoff (1893-1984)**

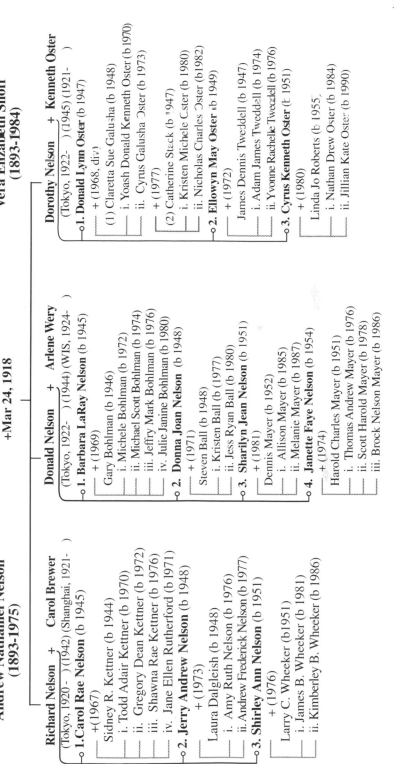

Richard Nelson + Carol Brewer
(Tokyo, 1920-) (1942) (Shanghai, 1921-)
- o 1. Carol Rae Nelson (b 1945)
  +(1967)
  Sidney R. Kettner (b 1944)
  - i. Todd Adair Kettner (b 1970)
  - ii. Gregory Dean Kettner (b 1972)
  - iii. Shawna Rae Kettner (b 1976)
  - iv. Jane Ellen Rutherford (b 1971)
- o 2. Jerry Andrew Nelson (b 1948)
  + (1973)
  Laura Dalgleish (b 1948)
  - i. Amy Ruth Nelson (b 1976)
  - ii. Andrew Frederick Nelson (b 1977)
- o 3. Shirley Ann Nelson (b 1951)
  + (1976)
  Larry C. Wheeker (b1951)
  - i. James B. Wheeker (b 1981)
  - ii. Kimberley B. Wheeker (b 1986)

Donald Nelson + Arlene Wery
(Tokyo, 1922-) (1944) (WIS, 1924-)
- o 1. Barbara LaRay Nelson (b 1945)
  + (1969)
  Gary Bohlman (b 1946)
  - i. Michele Bohlman (b 1972)
  - ii. Michael Scott Bohlman (b 1974)
  - iii. Jeffry Mark Bohlman (b 1976)
  - iv. Julie Janine Bohlman (b 1980)
- o 2. Donna Joan Nelson (b 1948)
  + (1971)
  Steven Ball (b 1948)
  - i. Kristen Ball (b 1977)
  - ii. Jess Ryan Ball (b 1980)
- o 3. Sharilyn Jean Nelson (b 1951)
  + (1981)
  Dennis Mayer (b 1952)
  - i. Allison Mayer (b 1985)
  - ii. Melanie Mayer (b 1987)
- 4. Janette Faye Nelson (b 1954)
  + (1974)
  Harold Charles Mayer (b 1951)
  - i. Thomas Andrew Mayer (b 1976)
  - ii. Scott Harold Mayer (b 1978)
  - iii. Brock Nelson Mayer (b 1986)

Dorothy Nelson + Kenneth Oster
(Tokyo, 1922-) (1945) (1921-)
- o 1. Donald Lynn Oster (b 1947)
  + (1968, div)
  (1) Claretta Sue Galusha (b 1948)
  - i. Yoash Donald Kenneth Oster (b 1970)
  - ii. Cyrus Galusha Oster (b 1973)
  + (1977)
  (2) Catherine Steck (b 1947)
  - i. Kristen Michele Oster (b 1980)
  - ii. Nicholas Charles Oster (b1982)
- o 2. Ellowyn May Oster (b 1949)
  + (1972)
  James Dennis Tweddell (b 1947)
  - i. Adam James Tweddell (b 1974)
  - ii. Yvonne Rachelle Tweddell (b 1976)
- o 3. Cyrus Kenneth Oster (b 1951)
  + (1980)
  Linda Jo Roberts (b 1955)
  - i. Nathan Drew Oster (b 1984)
  - ii. Jillian Kate Oster (b 1990)

APPENDIX I
ANDREW NELSON'S FAMILY WORK CHART

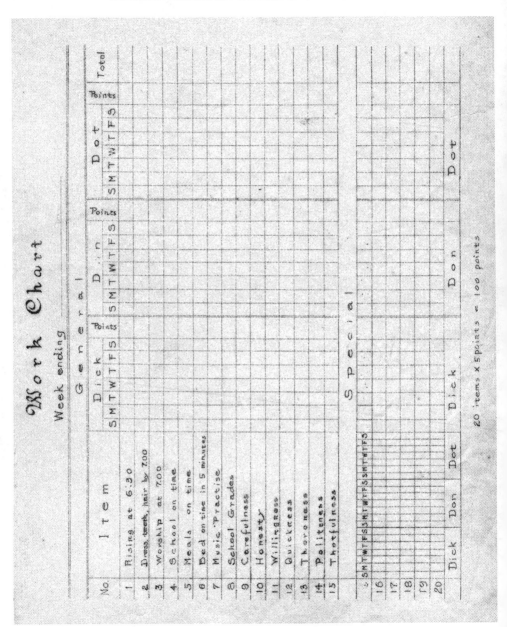

Andrew Nelson's well ordered life extended intimately into the lives of his three children. He personally designed the work chart for them. It challenged "Dick, Don, and Dot" at every level—physical, mental and spiritual. Moreover their achievements were assessed on a "commercial" scale.

APPENDIX II[1]

Japanese Prisoners of War in Bilibid Prison, Baptized into the SDA Church, Philippine Union College, October 29, 1949

NAME	RANK/DATE	SENTENCE & REMARKS
1. HANADA, Ishi	September 20, 1949	Hanging, Pardoned
2. HATAYAMA, Yoshini	June 13, 1949	Hanging
3. ICHIMURA, Isao	Major October 17, 1948	Hanging
4. INAMURA, Rokunogo	December, 1949	20 years in prison
5. ITO, Masayasu	Captain January 21, 1948	Hanging Innocent(a)[2]
6. KAGAMI, Masaji	Navy Officer February 19, 1949	Hanging
7. KATSUZAKI, Hideichi	July 29, 1948	20 years in prison
8. KOTOUME, Hisayoshi	August 27, 1948	30 years in prison
9. MINEO, Shizuhiko	Navy Officer February 19, 1949	Hanging Innocent(b)
10. NAKAMURA, Hideichi	Captain May 27, 1948	Hanging
11. OGAWA, Eitaro	Sergeant February 10, 1948	Hanging
12. OWARI, Saburo	1st Lieutenant October 17, 1948	Hanging
13. SAITO, Takao	April 27, 1948	Hanging
14. SATA, Takeshi	September 20, 1949	Life imprisonment
15. SEKINORI, Norimichi	Sergeant May 27, 1948	Hanging Innocent(a)
16. SUEO, A. E.	May 27, 1948	Hanging
17. TATOKORO, Minotaro, MD	Corporal September 20, 1949	Hanging
18. TANINAKA, Katanyeshi	1st Lieutenant September 15, 1948	Musketry Innocent(a)
19. TSUJI, Chyoichi	September 20, 1949	Life imprisonment

[1] M. S. Fajardo, Captain JAGS. Adm-o DPO, "Japanese Who Recently Were Baptized into Christianity."
[2] Matsuzaki, "The List of the Japanese Prisoners That Have been Condemned to Death in Spite of Their Being Innocent." Tr. by Andrew Nelson. nd.

APPENDIX III

Japanese Prisoners Wrongfully Sentenced to Death
by Hanging in Bilibid Prison
(Based on the research and classifications of Matsuzaki Hideichi)

NAME	DEGREE OF CERTAINTY	RANK
1. ABE, Sueo		
2. ARAO, Hatsuyoshi	c	1st Lieutenant
3. ETO, Toshitaka	c/a	Sergeant
4. HAMADA, Yoshi	c	1st Lieutenant
5. HANADA, Ishi		
6. HARADA, Shimpei	c	Major
7. HANAOKA, Michi	a	Navy Officer
8. HOSHINO, Takashi	a	Sgt. Major
9. ICHIMURA, Isao		
10. ICHINOSE, Haruo, MD	a	Navy Doctor
11. ITO, Masayasu	b	Captain
12. KOBAYASHI, Masataka	a	Warrant
13. KAGAMI, Masaji	b	Navy Officer
14. MINEO, Shizuhiko	b	Navy Officer
15. KUWABAEA, Tetsuo	b	Navy Officer
16. KUDO, Chushiro	a	Captain (already executed)
17. KOSE, Yasumasa	c	Navy Officer
18. KUWAHARA, Tetsuo		
19. MIKI, Iwao	a	Veterinary
20. MORI, Kenkichi	c	Sergeant
21. NAKAMURA, Hideichi	a	Captain
22. NAKANISHI, Shoji	a	Sergeant
23. OGAWA, Eitaro	?	Sergeant
24. OWARI, Saburo	b	1st Lieutenant
25. SAKUMA, Keiji	c	Sgt. Major
26. SASAKI, Haruo	a	1st Class Pvt.
27. SEKIMORI, Norimichi	a	Sergeant
28. SHIROTA, Gintaro		
29. SUZUKI, Misutada	a	Warrant Officer
30. TANINAKA, Katsuyoshi	c/a	1st Lieutenant
31. TSUBAKI, Takao	a	Navy Officer
32. UENO, Katsushiro	a	Sgt. Major
33. UENO, Masami	a	Navy Officer

APPENDIX IV
Tributes to Andrew Nelson (1975)

As a Member of Scholarly Organizations:
The Association of Japanese Teachers,
The Association of Chinese Teachers,
The Association of Asian Students,
The Riverside International Council, and
The International Council of Orientalists.

As a Writer, he authored books on a variety of subjects:

1. *"The Gist of Christian Education"*
   (with Dr. Reuben Manalaysay)

2. *"Food for Everyone"*
   (with Jacob Mittleider)

3. Three Japanese Dictionaries:
   For his Modern Reader's *"Japanese-English Character Dictionary"* He won first prize from the Society for the Promotion of Cultural Relations (1969). Also the Japan-International Library Award for his contribution to *"Japanese-American friendship"*. His doctoral dissertation on *"The Origin, History, and Present Status of the Temples of Japan"* (1938) represented very early scholarship on Japanese culture.

As a Colleague:

Two letters from Winston Clark, President, Far Eastern Division (1975)
To Dorothy Nelson-Oster:
"Your father is one of the great men that has served the church here in the Far East. He had complete optimism that carried him through some of the most difficult and trying experiences of his life. He was a man of tremendous vision, and, while this frequently brought him into conflict with people of a more practical nature, yet time always seemed to bear out his ideas.

He was not given to talking about other people. In this respect, he was a big man, and those of us who worked with him and observed this, liked him even better for it. We will always cherish his memory as a warm and close friend, for he was to us a source of tremendous inspiration, wonderful counsel, and great encouragement."

To Vera Nelson:
"Dr. Nelson was one of the great men who served the church here in the Far East so well, showing respect and admiration that increased with the passing years. He had the ability to look up and beyond the present problems,

and see what the work would require a decade or a generation beyond the present. This did much to strengthen the work here in the various parts of the Far East. A true mark of a great man, he was not critical of his fellow workers who criticized him. I always counted him as a real friend. There lingers behind in my mind a memory of one of the finest men I ever was privileged to know or to work with."

From the Mayor of Riverside, California:"He was a wonderful man who gave freely of his time to his fellow-men and his community."

From Elder Robert Pierson, President of the General Conference of Seventh-day Adventists: "He has been a strong leader and one who lived the church and gave his all for it."

From Elder Spangler, General Conference of Seventh-day Adventists: "He was such an inspiration to all who knew him. He had a vision and a tenacity rarely seen by people in the world today."

From Elder Paul Eldridge, Former President, Far Eastern Division:
"Here is a man who had no fears."

From Others:

"His life was of constant usefulness right to the end."

"He was such a wonderful and kind person who accomplished much work for the church and many people."

"We never knew anyone who made such good use of minutes/of time. He was always so intensely vital and active that he seemed immune to anything. He certainly made a big contribution to the work of the church."

"We have great respect for him, and we will never forget how really good he was to us."

"His workers described him as a kind and faithful man who had been loyal to his church."

"Andrew was such a dynamic person, and no other person was like him."

"Dr. Nelson is the only person that I've ever admired."

"What a tremendous job his *Japanese Character Dictionary* is, for it is a marvel."

"I am led to believe that the person of Dr. Nelson deserves most of the credit for selecting and establishing the School of the Light, Mountain View College."